HEALTHY
SLOW COOKER
cookbook

You might also like

The Slow Cooker Cookbook
Low-Carb Slow Cooker
Slow Cooker Family Classics
The Keto Slow Cooker
Slow Cooker: for Less
The Sugar-Free Family Cookbook
The Healthy Halogen Cookbook
Perfect Baking with Your Halogen Oven
Halogen Cooking for Two
The Everyday Halogen Family Cookbook
The Everyday Halogen Oven Cookbook
Eating to Beat Type 2 Diabetes

the
HEALTHY
SLOW COOKER
cookbook

SARAH FLOWER

ROBINSON

ROBINSON

First published in Great Britain in 2011 by Spring Hill,
an imprint of Constable & Robinson Ltd

This edition published in Great Britain in 2022 by Robinson

10 9 8 7 6 5 4 3 2

A CIP catalogue record for this book
is available from the British Library.

ISBN 978-1-47214-702-8

Illustrations by Firecatcher Creative
Produced for How To Books by Deer Park Productions, Tavistock, Devon
Typeset by TW Typesetting, Plymouth, Devon
Printed and bound in Great Britain by Bell & Bain Ltd

Papers used by Robinson are from well-managed forests
and other responsible sources

Robinson
An imprint of
Little, Brown Book Group
Carmelite House
50 Victoria Embankment
London EC4Y 0DZ

An Hachette UK Company
www.hachette.co.uk

www.littlebrown.co.uk

NOTE: The material contained in this book is set out in good faith for general guidance and
no liability can be accepted for loss or expense incurred as a result of relying in particular
circumstances on statements made in the book. Laws and regulations are complex and liable to
change, and readers should check the current position with relevant authorities before making
personal arrangements.

How To Books are published by Robinson, an imprint of Little, Brown Book Group.
We welcome proposals from authors who have first-hand experience of their subjects. Please
set out the aims of your book, its target market and its suggested contents in an email to
HowTo@littlebrown.co.uk

Contents

Weight

Metric	Imperial
25g	1oz
50g	2oz
75g	3oz
100g	4oz
150g	5oz
175g	6oz
200g	7oz
225g	8oz
250g	9oz
300g	10oz
350g	12oz
400g	14oz
450g	1lb

Oven temperatures

Celsius	Fahrenheit
110°C	225°F
120°C	250°F
140°C	275°F
150°C	300°F
160°C	325°F
180°C	350°F
190°C	375°F
200°C	400°F
220°C	425°F
230°C	450°F
240°C	475°F

Liquids

Metric	Imperial	US cup
5ml	1 tsp	1 tsp
15ml	1 tbsp	1 tbsp
50ml	2fl oz	3 tbsp
60ml	$2\frac{1}{2}$fl oz	$\frac{1}{4}$ cup
75ml	3fl oz	$\frac{1}{3}$ cup
100ml	4fl oz	scant $\frac{1}{2}$ cup
125ml	$4\frac{1}{2}$fl oz	$\frac{1}{2}$ cup
150ml	5fl oz	$\frac{2}{3}$ cup
200ml	7fl oz	scant 1 cup
250ml	9fl oz	1 cup
300ml	$\frac{1}{2}$pt	$1\frac{1}{4}$ cups
350ml	12fl oz	$1\frac{1}{3}$ cups
400ml	$\frac{3}{4}$pt	$1\frac{3}{4}$ cups
500ml	17fl oz	2 cups
600ml	1pt	$2\frac{1}{2}$ cups

Measurements

Metric	Imperial
5cm	2in
10cm	4in
13cm	5in
15cm	6in
18cm	7in
20cm	8in
25cm	10in
30cm	12in

Introduction

In 2010, I wrote *Slow Cook, Fast Food*, which was a popular slow cook and one pot recipe book. This book has taken my favourite slow cook recipes along with plenty of new ones and given them a healthy twist – so now, you can enjoy the simplicity of slow cooking whilst watching your weight and following a healthier lifestyle. I hope you enjoy it.

The joy of slow cook

Slow cookers have been around since the 1970s. At the time, they were seen to be the perfect way to tenderise cheap pieces of meat, and to create simple and wholesome meals for busy families. Our desire to be thrifty, plus create wholesome meals has seen a resurrection for the slow cooker . . . and about time to I think!

The key to successful slow cooker dishes is to be organised. Slow cook meals need to be planned in advance – there is no point coming home after a busy day and then thinking of putting something in the slow cooker. You need to organise your life and in most cases prepare the food in the morning or night before. Don't panic, this does not have to be as arduous as it sounds. Around 15–30 minutes maximum spent in preparation and you will have a wonderful, nutritious and warm meal waiting for you when you come home from work. I love the simplicity of the slow cooker. You fill it with your ingredients (no need to sauté, brown off or similar unless you want to brown the meat), pop the lid on and walk away for 4–10 hours depending on the setting, and because the slow cooker cooks slowly, the nutrients are preserved. Because the food is cooked slowly, it won't spoil if you want to delay dinner for half an hour – invaluable if like me, everyone seems to call just as I am about to serve dinner.

For those of us concerned about saving money – the slow cooker claims to use no more electricity than a light bulb. Fill it with cheaper cuts of meat, cooked slowly, to produce tender and tasty dishes. You can also make delicious soups, puddings and even conserves and chutneys. I love making chutneys. There is something magical about using up any unwanted ingredients and creating something special. Chutney making brings out the domestic goddess in me – I just wish I had a Victorian-style pantry to place them all in.

Enjoy experimenting with your slow cooker. I have by trial and error, perfected cakes, sponge puddings and delicious mugs of hot chocolate brownies. Vegetables, particularly root vegetables, take the longest time to cook. Seafood, dairy and frozen vegetables only need to be added in the last half hour or hour of cooking. Fresh herbs can lose their flavour so it is often best to use dried herbs and only add fresh herbs in the last half an hour of cooking time. Your slow cooker should come with an instruction booklet which can explain this in more detail or have a look at the next chapter for a more detailed explanation.

Don't forget your slow cooker at Christmas, you can steam your Christmas pudding, prepare you mulled wine and prepare your gammon joint. Any leftover turkey can be turned into a delicious casserole, leaving you time to sit back and enjoy Christmas without slaving over a hot stove.

DISCLAIMER

The temperatures and timings listed in the recipes are guides as slow cookers can vary, so get to know your slow cooker. Older slow cookers or very basic ones can often cook a little hotter than they should. If your slow cooker is bubbling away and evaporating liquid, it may be best to cook on low rather than high and opt for the lower end of the recommended cooking time. If you don't have an auto-timing switch, which ensures the slow cooker turns to warm when you have reached your specified cooking time, you may want to consider a timing plug, especially if you are out all day and can't monitor your slow cooker.

How to Use your Slow Cooker

Slow cookers gained popularity in the 1970s, but the principle of slow cooking goes back hundreds of years – think of the large stock pots seen dangling from ranges! Slow cookers were seen to revolutionise the kitchen, they could create wholesome meals ready for your return after a busy day. It was incredibly popular, but sadly became relegated to kitchen cupboards as we moved into the Thatcher years of 'loads of money' when our need to live a frugal life ceased to have relevance. Cheaper cuts of meats ceased to be popular so there seemed to be no real reason to keep the slow cooker in our kitchens. The microwave and processed food became the housewife's choice for a busy home and the poor slow cooker ceased to inspire. Thankfully we are now seeing a revival as we realise that these clever machines not only can save us time, they are also superior nutritionally.

Where to buy

You can buy slow cookers from as little as £15 from your supermarket, electrical store or Argos. If you are a member of Freecycle, you may find someone is giving one away, or you could put out a wanted request. Bootsales are also a great place for picking up a bargain. I have a crock pot and a stainless steel slow cooker. I know it sounds extravagant, but sometimes I am cooking two dishes at the same time; either a dessert and a main meal, or two main meals if I am trying to get ahead or use up fresh ingredients.

Size matters

Think about the size of the machine. Some look quite big but when you take it apart and look at the actual size of the stock pot, you may be shocked. If you are cooking for a large family or like to plan ahead and freeze food, you may be better off spending more money and investing in a larger machine. Go to an electrical store where you can actually view the machines – even if you don't buy from them, it will give you an idea of the machines on sale and what your requirements are.

To sauté or not to sauté

Recipes often tell you to sauté the onions or brown the meat. I have tried with and without and to be honest I really did not notice much difference in the taste, just colour sometimes. If you are cooking whole chicken, for example, remember that this will not brown, so may look a bit unappealing. Coating the meat with flour can also help if you want a thicker sauce – remember the slow cooker doesn't lose much liquid, so you may find you need to thicken the dish until you get used to the way your machine works – they are all different! If you prefer to brown your meat or sauté your vegetables before placing in the slow cooker, you can use your hob. I use a large sauté pan, add some vegetables and the meat, and if I want to hurry things along, I may add all the ingredients and bring to the boil before transferring to the slow cooker. You may find that your slow cooker has a sauté facility, others come with hob-proof dishes, allowing you to transfer from one source to the other. You will need to refer to your manufacturer's instructions for more information.

Cooking techniques

All slow cookers will come with full manufacturer's instructions, recipe suggestions and even a useful helpline if you get stuck. I strongly advise you read these booklets before using your machine. Here are some reminders:

- Some cookers need to be preheated, which can take up to 15 minutes, others heat up fast so you may not need to do this (refer to your manufacturer's recommendations).

- As a general rule of thumb, one hour in a conventional oven equates to 2–3 hours on high in a slow cooker, or 6 hours on low heat. Some slow cookers have an auto setting – this basically means it heats up on high quickly then when it reaches temperature, reverts to low for remainder of the cooking. This helps food, especially meat, reach a safe temperature quickly. Some machines have a warm setting which is useful if the food has reached its maximum cooking time and you just want to keep it warm, but really, the low setting is enough and food can cook for 10 hours without starting to spoil.

- You may need to adjust the liquid content of your dish depending on your personal taste but remember you do need liquid in order to cook the food – all food must be submersed in the liquid before cooking – potatoes especially may bob around on top and go black, so push them into the stock. Your manufacturer's guidelines should detail the minimum and maximum fill levels for your machine. The slow cooker does not evaporate liquid as much as other cooking methods so you may need to thicken the soups or casseroles – to do this, add 1–2 teaspoons of cornflower to a small amount of water, mix thoroughly before adding to the food. Turn the temperature to high and cook for 30 minutes until it thickens. Adding more water or stock is simple and can be done at any stage.

- The key point to remember about slow cooking is that once you start cooking, you shouldn't keep removing the lid as this reduces the temperature and then it takes longer for the slow cooker to get back up to the required temperature. The outer edge of the lid forms a seal – sometimes this may spit or bubble out, but this is quite normal. Only remove it when absolutely necessary – ideally just when it finishes cooking or if necessary, in the last 30 minutes of cooking to add key ingredients. If you are the sort of person who likes to keep an eye on things – opt for a slow cooker with a glass lid (though this is not foolproof as they do get steamed up!).

- Always defrost any frozen ingredients thoroughly before placing them in the slow cooker, especially meat. The slow cooker is designed to cook safely at low temperatures. However, if your cooker does not maintain the required heat, it could increase the risk of food poisoning caused by the spread of bacteria. Frozen foods such as peas, sweetcorn, prawns and other quick cook vegetables should only be added in the last 30 minutes of cooking time.

- When adding liquids such as stock or water, to maintain the temperature, it is better to use warm liquids (not boiling) rather than cold.

- Pasta should only be added in the last 30 minutes of cooking time as it goes very soggy and breaks up for longer cooking times.

- Fresh herbs can be used but tend to lose the intense flavours for longer cooking times. If I am using fresh herbs, I add in the last 30 minutes of cooking.

- Vegetables, especially root vegetables, take much longer to cook than meat. You can speed up the process by sautéing the vegetables prior to adding to the dish, or simply chopping them into smaller chunks. Make sure the vegetables are thoroughly immersed in the stock – ideally on the base as this is the hottest area.

Cakes

I have made cakes in the slow cooker and these have been really tasty, though sometimes can be a different texture from oven baked. I think it is more personal taste. Some may not like the moist, almost bread pudding type texture of the fruit cakes. I have cooked cakes simply by placing the cake dish in the slow cooker and adding water to the base creating a bain marie – which works well with sponge puddings and Christmas pudding. The most popular recipe in my house is the hot chocolate orange brownie mugs.

Freezing

If you want to get ahead, why not double up the recipe and freeze some. To do this make sure you remove the dish from the slow cook and allow it to chill thoroughly before freezing. You can buy special freezer bags for more liquid meals such as soups or casseroles. These can be more expensive than normal freezer bags – one tip is to place a normal freezer bag in a bowl. Add the food and freeze – removing the bag from the bowl once it is frozen. Make sure it is completely defrosted before reheating – you can reheat in a saucepan, but please make sure it is thoroughly reheated before serving.

Healthy Eating Tips

The food we eat is generally seen in three categories (protein, carbohydrates and fats). Food also contains minerals, vitamins, phytonutrients, antioxidants, fibre and water.

Protein – Protein is essential for the body. Imagine a brick wall – protein is the wall, but each brick is an amino acid. These amino acids (and there are loads of them) play a role in everything within our body – from digestion (forming digestive enzymes) to neurotransmitters in the brain. Without protein we would not survive.

You can find protein in lots of foods but the strongest sources are meat, fish, beans (such as chick peas, haricot beans, etc.), lentils, some dairy and eggs. One of the great things about protein for dieters is when carbohydrates are eaten with protein, it slows down the absorption of the carbohydrates, which in turn reduces the rise in blood sugar, which in turn reduces excess glucose converting into fat and it also keeps you fuller for longer.

Carbohydrates – Carbohydrates are essential for our bodies – which is why people on the Atkins diet have so many health problems when the reduce their carbohydrates dramatically. Carbohydrates are converted in the liver into glucose. Glucose is the fuel for our body – cells need it to survive. Glucose is pushed out of your liver and enters your blood stream. It is dangerous to have glucose in your blood stream, so your body produces insulin to help get rid of it. It is then transported to muscle where it is stored as glycogen, or more commonly it converts the glucose to fat. When glucose remains in the bloodstream too long, the sugar actually coats the red blood cell, and that makes the blood cell stiff. That interferes with blood circulation, causing cholesterol to build up on the inside lining of the blood vessel. It can take years for the damage to become apparent, but smaller, more fragile blood vessels such as those in the eyes, kidneys and feet are most at risk.

If you eat a high carbohydrate diet, you cause high levels of glucose to enter the blood stream – more insulin to be produced and more conversion to fat. If this continues, your body will stop listening to the signals to produce insulin and you will start to develop type 2 diabetes.

Carbohydrates fall into two categories – refined carbohydrates and complex carbohydrates. Refined carbohydrates are the foods that have been altered – normally meaning the goodness has been taken out. Think of white flour, white pasta, sugar, and the multitude of foods that contain white flour and sugar. Most nutritionists now believe that carbohydrates are responsible for obesity. Calorie controlled diets are often high in carbohydrates because carbohydrates have lower calories than fat, which helps explain why people say they can't shift the fat around the middle even after following strict diets. When you become insulin resistant, your body also stops breaking down fats already stored in the body, therefore once fat, you stay fat until you address the glucose situation.

If you think of the Western diet, it is mainly high in refined carbohydrates and bad fats – both of which convert within the body to fat. It is hardly surprising that obesity is on the rise.

Complex carbohydrates, on the other hand, are good for you – they are the wholegrains, brown pasta, brown rice, nuts, seeds – basically whole foods. Complex carbohydrates are much slower to digest as they have additional nutrients including protein and have a high quantity of fibre, all of which slows down the absorption of the carbohydrates, meaning you are not only fuller for longer, but you also avoid those nasty sugar highs and lows shown above.

Fats – Our bodies needs fat. Good fats are used in the body for almost every function. We actually have little receptors on our tongue which tell us when our bodies need good fat – so when you crave your fatty chips, you really are wanting fat, but sadly opting for a bad one and not the good one!

Good fats – These are called Essential fatty acids – omega 3 and omega 6.

Omega 3 – This is the granddaddy of good fats – these are vital for optimum health. These good fats are found in oily fish, nuts, seeds (and oils from nuts and seeds). Your body needs these to function properly. They are used by the brain (the brain is made from 60%

fat), nerves, hormones immune system, immunity, skin and heart – what is left, if any, is then stored. A diet rich in omega 3 also helps combat diabetes, Alzheimer's, ageing, cancer, reverse the effects of heart disease, prevent arthritis and can even prevent wrinkles! It also helps your metabolism break down stored fat, so eating good fats really can make you thinner!

Omega 6 – This is found in seeds such as sunflower and sesame seeds, pumpkin seeds (or oils from these). It is particularly good for the skin and maintaining hormone balance. Omega 6 deficiency can manifest as arthritis, alopecia, mental health problems, eczema, liver or kidney degeneration, poor healing and even miscarriage.

Bad fats – Saturated fats – these found in meat, some fish and dairy products, are bad as 100% of saturated fats are stored as fat or used as energy. An average child consumes over 317kg (700lb) of saturated fat, the equivalent of 1,314 packets of lard between the ages of 6 and 16.
   You also get really baddies like transfats and hydrogenated fats. Found in deep fried foods, burned or browned fats, margarine's, processed meats. Avoid these if you can.

Antioxidants – These are normally found in fruit and vegetables. The most common are berries, broccoli, onion, garlic, sweet potato. Try to include these in your diet as they help combat cellular damage caused by oxidants (otherwise known as free radicals). They also boost your immune system.

Phytonutrients – These are a name for special nutrients that enhance health – again mainly found in fruit and vegetables and some whole foods. Research suggests that some phytonutrients have been shown to reverse some cancers – green tea, garlic, red onions, raspberries, turmeric are particularly powerful. Broccoli is especially good for hormone related cancers.

Fibre – This is essential for good digestion and for keeping your bowel healthy. It also slows down the digestive process helping you stay fuller for longer and helps your body to break down fat stores.

Vitamins and minerals – There is a huge variety of vitamins and minerals – again whole foods and fruit and vegetables are the purest forms. Boiling destroys most vitamins which is why steaming, stir fry and slow cooking are best.

Food swaps

Sugar – Instead try to use more xylitol, Stevia (there are new blends in supermarkets now which are either all Stevia or half and half), Sweet Freedom Syrup (dark or light) or Groovy Food company do a Agave Nectar syrup which is also low GI (low Glycaemic Index which means it does not peak your blood sugar levels).

Butter – Butter is actually okay, most nutritionists prefer you to use it in moderation rather than manufactured margarines. Stork is fine in cakes. You can buy a pure margarine if you prefer – I would not be too concerned about this, just make sure you don't overuse it.

Milk – Skimmed or semi-skimmed is fine. If you are making milky puddings or sauces, it may be prudent to swap to skimmed milk.

Chocolate – Swap to dark chocolate as it still gives you the endorphin boost (feel good factor) but is also packed with antioxidants and phytonutrients. Some nutritionists recommend that their clients eat one or two squares a day as a medicinal boost! Milk chocolate is high in sugar and fat and has very little cocoa rich content so does not have the same health benefits as dark.

Oils – Remember oil is good for you! Choose oily fish, nuts and seeds (linseeds, sunflower seeds, pumpkin seeds, etc.). Oil is destroyed with light, heat and oxygen so buy good oils that highlight the omega 3/6 content. They must be in dark bottles and you must store in the fridge. Don't heat it as you will destroy the nutrients. Use it in salad dressings – you can also use in on jacket potatoes or warm foods as a topping as long as you eat it straight away. For cooking, use either coconut oil (which is in a jar and solid mass until heated – it has amazing health promoting properties!) or fill a spray container with olive oil.

Fruit and vegetables – Unlimited – steam or stir fry is best as it does not destroy the nutrients. If you are cooking casseroles or stews – low heat for longer periods of time retains the nutrients making a much healthier meal – slow cookers are fantastic for healthy options.

Meat – Ideally don't have more than three meat evening meals per week, but if you do eat more, try chicken or even better, turkey as it is lower fat. Meat is high in saturated fat (that gooey stuff that can clog up your arteries). When choosing meat, opt for the leanest best quality.

Fish – Try to eat at least three fish dishes per week, ideally oily fish (salmon, herring, mackerel, sardines, tuna, pilchards, trout). If you don't like oily fish, I would advise a fish oil supplement, ideally Krill oil as it is the best on the market and has amazing health benefits for diabetes, heart disease and even cancer.

Pulses, beans – Lentils, pulses and beans are really good for you. They contain high levels of protein, fibre and are nutrient rich. They are also cheap to buy and great for bulking out meals (red lentils are the ones that dissolve almost to nothing but packed with nutrients and high in magnesium). Beans are particularly good for the digestion.

Cream – Use creme fraiche (but use low fat as standard creme fraiche is as high in fat as cream), natural fat-free Greek yoghurt, quark, mascarpone. Stir a little vanilla essence or paste to create a sweeter flavour – you can also add a teaspoon of icing sugar or the syrups mentioned above.

Biscuits – Opt for homemade flapjack (made with the sugar-free syrups mentioned above), Nairns oakcakes (available in sweet flavours such as chocolate chip, mixed spice, fruit and ginger). Wholegrain crackers are pretty much guilt-free – it is the toppings you need to be aware of – Laughing Cow purple one is virtually fat-free.

Cheese – If you want cheese, opt for mature (especially when cooking as you use less to create the flavour). You can now buy lighter cheese which is up to 30% less fat – Cathedral City do one which is very nice but there are lots on the market now.

Cut the fizz

A two-litre bottle of cola contains more than 40 teaspoons of sugar! Fizzy drinks also dilute your natural stomach acid and can prevent correct absorption of nutrients. Avoid these, especially when eating a meal – far better to sip still water when eating.

Breakfast – don't avoid breakfast!

Ideally porridge is a great breakfast, especially if you want to be fuller for longer. Use the sugar alternative above or top with fresh fruit. Oats are amazing – they grab toxins from the stomach and remove them so ideal after recovering from a tummy bug or when you are nauseous. They help reduce high blood pressure, cholesterol and aid digestion.

There is nothing wrong with having grilled lean bacon, ham or salmon for breakfast, alongside some scrabbled or poached eggs and grilled tomatoes.

Always opt for seeded, wholegrain bread or rye bread.

Good food rules

- Home cooked is always healthier than shop bought.

- Low salt.

- Low fat (removing any visible fat from meat, cutting out processed, junk foods, avoid frying foods, avoid too much dairy).

- Eat more oily fish (at least 2–3 times a week).

- Rich in fruit and vegetables.

- Eat more nuts and seeds!

- Wholegrains – avoid white processed refined carbohydrates.

- Keep sugar to a minimum.

- Use pulses (helps keep cholesterol low, good bowel health and rich in nutrients).

- Drink plenty of water (we often confuse dehydration for hunger pangs).

- Eat well – don't avoid meals. Little and often is better. Don't go longer than 3–4 hours without having something to eat.

Recipes

- Most recipes can be adapted to make them healthier. Take simple steps to convert a recipe – read through the recipe first to familiarise yourself, then make some changes.

- If it uses oil to fry/brown/sauté, swap this for a spray of your olive oil or even better, a little of the coconut oil.

- Only use lean meat where applicable – or swap for Quorn which cholesterol free, has 75% less saturated fat than lean beef and is a rich source of protein.

- If you are making a soup or casserole, use a little less meat but bulk out with beans or pulses – this will add nutrients and cut down on your saturated fat.

- Steam instead of boil.

- Add nutrients – if you are doing a mash topping, use half sweet potato – this will add nutrients and antioxidants without changing the flavour. Grate carrot into your spaghetti bolognaise, add red lentils to soups, casseroles, shepherd's pie, etc.

- Use herbs and spices in your foods – chilli speeds up metabolism; turmeric has anti-cancer properties and is a great anti-inflammatory (particularly great for arthritis); cinnamon helps lower cholesterol, unclog arteries and balance blood sugar levels; parsley, known to help unclog arteries, help pass kidney stones and even help with hearing problems; garlic is anti-viral, anti-fungal and anti-bacterial. It has also shown to boost the immune system, help with heart disease and has anti-cancer properties.

CHAPTER 3

Slow Cook Soups

Soups are bursting with nutrients. Quick and easy, they can be used as a quick snack or a nutritious meal; they are cheap too. Kids can be tempted with a side helping of toasted soldiers, hot pitta bread with hummus or even healthy potato wedges. If you or your child has a packed lunch, why not invest in a small flask and fill with your homemade soup – perfect to fill up and warm the body, especially during the winter months.

Most soups can be frozen. You can buy special bags for liquids, but I cheat. Use a freezer bag and place this inside a plastic bowl or container. Fill with your soup and freeze. Once frozen you can remove the bowl and tie the bag. Don't forget to label and date the bags!

Soup-making advice

Stock

Stock cubes can be quite overpowering and also high in salt. Ideally use homemade stock or even just water and fresh herbs, allowing the natural flavours to rule. If you prefer stock cubes, why not try the low salt varieties – much better for your health.

Pureeing soups

Some people like a chunky soup, others like a smooth soup. It is purely personal taste. When pureeing a soup, I use an electric hand blender (or some call it a stick blender). It is simple to use and saves on washing up and messy transfer to a liquidiser (though make sure the end of the blender is fully submerged in the soup or you will end up with it everywhere). For a really fine soup, you can filter through a sieve.

Chunky soups

Some chunky soups may benefit from a thicker stock/sauce. To do this, simply remove about a quarter of the soup and puree, then add back to the soup.

Liquid

You may need to adjust the liquid content of your soup depending on your personal taste. The slow cooker does not evaporate liquid as much as other cooking methods so you may need to thicken the soups – to do this, add 1–2 teaspoons of cornflower to a small amount of water, mix thoroughly before adding to the soup. Turn the temperature to high and cook for 15–30 minutes until thick – alternatively you could remove some of the chunky soup and puree. Adding more water or stock is simple and can be done at any stage.

Pulses and beans

Adding pulses and beans not only is a cheap way to bulk out a meal, but it also adds essential nutrients to your dish and can keep you fuller for longer.

Creams

Creams, milk, Greek yoghurt and creme fraiche can separate when cooked in a slow cooker for long periods, so best to add this just before serving.

Note For all of the recipes in this chapter, **if your slow cooker needs to be preheated, turn it on 15 minutes before using.** Refer to your manufacturer's instructions for more information on your specific model temperatures.

Tomato, Pepper and Sweet Potato Soup

Ingredients:

2 red onions, diced

2 red peppers, diced

1 sweet potato, diced

3 cloves of garlic, chopped

250–300g vine tomatoes, diced

½ tsp dried thyme

400ml low salt vegetable stock or water

Seasoning to taste

This soup is rich in lycopene and rich in antioxidants. Lycopene from tomatoes is more available and better absorbed by our body when the tomatoes are cooked.

- Cut the vegetables into equal size so you get a more even cook.

- Add all ingredients. Make sure the stock is hot when adding as this will keep the temperature.

- Cook on low for 6–8 hours or if you want a faster meal, turn to high for 4–5 hours.

- Liquidise gently using an electric stick blender (this way you avoid washing up a liquidiser).

- Serve with a drizzle of chilli oil.

Serves 4

Chunky Winter Vegetable and Lentil Soup

A wholesome soup, perfect for a winter's day or when you fancy a more filling soup. This is a great soup to use up any vegetables you may have.

Ingredients:
1 red onion, finely chopped
1 large carrot, diced
2 sweet potatoes, diced
1 leek, finely chopped
1 parsnip, diced
1 potato, diced
2 sticks of celery, diced
1 litre of low salt or homemade vegetable or chicken stock
2 cloves of garlic, crushed
1 bay leaf
75g red lentils
½ tsp dried parsley

- Remember to cut the vegetables into equal size so you get a more even cook.

- Add all ingredients. Make sure the stock is hot as this will keep the temperature.

- Cook on low for 8–10 hours or if you want a faster meal, turn to high for 5–6 hours.

- Leave chunky or puree if you prefer. I like to remove two thirds of the soup, puree the remaining third and then return to the chunky soup – this creates a creamy base for the chunky soup.

NB: I have avoided using swede in this recipe as I find it overpowers the flavour, but if you like swede, feel free to add some.

Health fact: This recipe delivers at least 2 portions of your 5 a day, and as it is packed with allium vegetables (red onions, garlic, leeks), it can help protect your joints from deterioration. The added lentils give you protein, with magnesium, biotin, zinc and iron.

Chicken, Cumin and Harissa Soup

Ingredients:
1 red onion, finely chopped
2–3 cloves of garlic, finely chopped
½ red pepper, finely chopped
1 tsp ground cumin
1 tsp paprika
2–3 tsp Harissa paste
1 tin chickpeas, drained
1 tin chopped tomatoes
400g chicken fillets, diced (thigh gives a nicer flavour)
800ml low salt or homemade chicken stock
Freshly chopped coriander
Dollop of natural yoghurt or creme fraiche

This is a lovely warming soup. The Harissa paste is one of my favourites. This needs to be left chunky so make sure you chop everything evenly.

- Add all ingredients apart from the fresh coriander (which you can add later). Make sure the chicken stock is hot when adding as this will keep the temperature.

- Turn your slow cooker to Auto and cook for 6–8 hours. If you don't have an auto setting, I would advise bringing the dish up to temperature in a saucepan before transferring to the slow cooker as it contains raw chicken. Cook on low for 6–8 hours or if you want a faster meal, turn to high for 4 hours. Add the fresh coriander 20 minutes before serving.

- To serve, add remaining coriander and a dollop of natural yoghurt or creme fraiche.

Healthy swap: Make sure your remove any fat from the chicken, including skin. If you want a lower fat version of this dish, you can swap the chicken breast for turkey. Turkey is a good source of protein but also carnosine, which research suggests, can help to slow down the ageing process.

Serves 4–6

Spicy Squash and Sweet Potato Soup

I love this soup. It is packed with nutrients, tastes delicious and has a lovely kick. Serve with warm crusty bread and hummus.

- Your slow cooker will need to be on high for the first part of this recipe. Preheat 10–15 minutes.

- When the slow cooker is on high, add the coconut oil, chilli, garlic, onion, and spices. Leave for 10 minutes whilst you cut the vegetables. This will help release the flavour of the spices.

- Add all the remaining ingredients. Make sure the stock is hot when adding as this will keep the temperature.

- Cook on low for 6–8 hours or if you want a faster meal, continue to cook on high for 4–5 hours.

- Using your stick blender, blend until smooth. Season to taste.

- Serve with a swirl of chilli oil.

Healthy tip: Sweet potatoes are packed with carotenoids, vitamin C, potassium and fibre.

Ingredients:
½ tsp coconut oil
1-2 chillies, finely chopped
1 onion, diced
1 stick of celery, diced
2 cloves of garlic, roughly chopped
½ tsp cumin seeds
½ tsp chilli powder
½ tsp smoked paprika
1 small squash, peeled, seeded and cut into chunks
2-3 sweet potatoes, peeled and cut into chunks
1 carrot, peeled and cut into chunks
700ml hot low salt vegetable stock
Swirl of chilli oil

Creamy Pea Soup

Ingredients:

1 onion, finely chopped

1 leek, finely chopped

2 sticks of celery, finely chopped

500g frozen or fresh peas

750ml low salt vegetable or chicken stock

Black pepper

Handful of fresh mint leaves, finely chopped

½ tsp dried mint

2-3 heaped tbsp low fat creme fraiche or fat-free Greek yoghurt

This is a really nice soup, quick and easy. On high, this can be ready in 2 hours. I usually recommend red onions in most dishes as they have a higher nutrients and antioxidants, however, in this case it looks better to use standard onions.

- Add all ingredients apart from the mint leaves and creme fraiche/yoghurt. Make sure the stock is hot when adding as this will keep the temperature.

- Cook on low for 4–6 hours or if you want a faster meal, turn to high for 2–4 hours.

- In the last 20–30 minutes, add the mint leaves and ½ tsp dried mint and stir well. Taste and add more black pepper if needed.

- Just prior to serving, whizz with your blender before stirring in the creme fraiche or yoghurt. Serve immediately. Garnish with mint leaves.

Healthy swap: Low fat creme fraiche is higher in fat than fat-free Greek yoghurt. If you are watching your weight, opt for the Greek yoghurt. This holds its consistency in cooking – don't be tempted to use low fat natural yoghurt as it is runnier and won't work as well. Avoid adding salt – opt for low salt stock. The celery helps create a more salty flavour.

Serves 4

Pear and Celeriac Soup

Celeriac is a good source of fibre, is packed with potassium, phosphorus, vitamin C and B6.

- Remember to cut the vegetables into equal size so you get a more even cook.

- Add all ingredients. Make sure the stock is hot when adding as this will keep the temperature.

- Cook on low for 6–8 hours or if you want a faster meal, turn to high for 3–4 hours.

- Using your stick blender (or liquidiser) whizz until smooth. Stir in the creme fraiche and add the chopped chives.

- Serve immediately.

Healthy swap: Fat-free Greek yoghurt is a healthier choice than low fat creme fraiche – stir in for a creamy soup.

Ingredients:
1 onion, chopped
2cm knuckle of ginger, chopped
4 pears, peeled and diced
1 small celeriac, peeled and diced
400ml low salt vegetable stock or water
Black pepper
Small handful of freshly chopped parsley (or 1 tsp dried)
2 tbsp low fat creme fraiche or 0% fat natural Greek yoghurt
Few sprigs of fresh chives

Carrot and Coriander Soup

Ingredients:
1 large onion, chopped
1 clove garlic, crushed
400g carrots, diced
1 stick of celery, diced
2 tsp ground coriander
1 tsp ground cumin
750ml low salt vegetable
    stock or water
Black pepper
Small handful freshly chopped
    coriander leaves

This recipe is a family favourite but also packed with nutrients. A rich source of vitamin A and high in carotenoids.

- Remember to cut the vegetables into equal size so you get a more even cook.

- Add all ingredients. Make sure the stock is hot when adding as this will keep the temperature.

- Cook on low for 8–10 hours or if you want a faster meal, turn to high for 5–6 hours.

- Liquidise the soup, adding more liquid if necessary. Season to taste and reheat gently. Serve garnished with a few chopped coriander leaves.

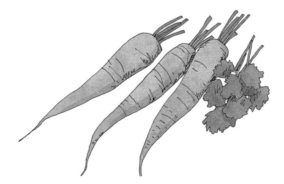

Serves 3–4

Chilli, Prawn and Noodle Soup

I have shamelessly pinched this recipe from a friend of mine. She first discovered this recipe online and has since adapted it. It is a big hit with her family and friends, so I hope you enjoy it.

- Add all ingredients apart from the noodles and coriander. Make sure the stock is hot when adding as this will keep the temperature.

- Turn your slow cooker to high and cook for 2 hours. Add the noodles and coriander and cook for another 20 minutes before serving.

Ingredients:
1 bunch of spring onions, finely chopped
2–3 cloves of garlic, crushed
1 chilli, finely chopped
1–2 inch knuckle of ginger, finely chopped
200g tiger prawns, shelled
75g creamed coconut
500ml fish stock
4–6 tsp fish sauce
100g fresh rice noodles
Handful of fresh coriander

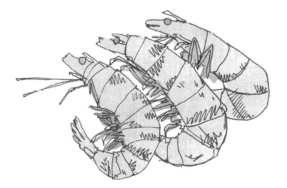

Serves 4–6

Wholesome Ham and Vegetable Soup

Ingredients:
1 red onion, finely chopped
2 carrots, diced
1 sweet potato, diced
1 white potato, diced
75g soup mix
300g chopped ham (in chunks)
750ml low salt vegetable or
    chicken stock
½ tsp dried parsley
Black pepper
Small handful freshly chopped
    parsley

You will need to use thick ham chunks for this soup. The added soup mix and vegetables ensure this is a balanced and nutritious meal.

- Remove the fat from the ham. Prepare the vegetables – remember to cut the vegetables into equal size so you get a more even cook.

- Add all ingredients apart from the fresh parsley. Make sure the stock is hot when adding as this will keep the temperature.

- Cook on low for 6–8 hours or if you want a faster meal, turn to high for 4–5 hours.

- Half an hour before serving, add the freshly chopped parsley. Season to taste.

- This is a chunky soup – if you want to make it slightly thicker, remove up to a third of the soup and puree this. Stir it back into the chunky soup. This will make a creamy base to the chunky soup.

Healthy swap: If you want to avoid saturated fat from the ham, you can remove this and just have a wholesome vegetable soup. If you are opting for the ham, make sure any visible fat is removed before adding to the dish.

Serves 4–6

Sweet Potato, Carrot and Parsnip Soup

A delicious soup. The recipe does not use additional herbs as it allows the natural flavours to come through. Freshly chopped parsley or a tablespoon of dried is enough to make this soup yummy.

Ingredients:
1 large leek, sliced
2 celery sticks, chopped
3-4 sweet potatoes, cubed
2-3 carrots, cubed
1 large parsnip, cubed
700ml low salt vegetable
   stock
15ml fresh chopped parsley
Fresh ground black pepper to
   taste

- Remember to cut the vegetables into equal size so you get a more even cook.

- Add all ingredients. Make sure the stock is hot when adding as this will keep the temperature.

- Turn your slow cooker to low for 8 hours.

- If you want to thicken the soup, remove about a quarter of the cooled soup and liquid and liquidise until smooth. Return liquidised soup to the slow cooker and heat before serving.

- Serve sprinkled with parsley garnish.

Healthy swap: If you want a soup which will fill you for longer, add some beans, such a borlotti or cannellini beans or a handful of dried red lentils. Note, if you add lentils you may have to add more stock.

Serves 4

Tomato and Chilli Soup

Ingredients:
1 red onion, finely chopped
2 cloves garlic, crushed
1-2 chillies, depending on
  personal preference, finely
  chopped
800g fresh tomatoes, peeled
  and finely chopped
2 tsp sundried tomato puree
50g sundried tomatoes
Half stick celery – finely
  chopped
450ml water
1 heaped tsp paprika
Black pepper to taste
Drizzle of chilli oil

Tomato soup never fails to cheer me up – it is like a hug in a bowl or mug. Chillies are not only delicious but also help speed up your metabolism. If you don't fancy the heat, just omit the chillies.

- Remember to cut the vegetables into equal size so you get a more even cook.

- Add all ingredients. Make sure the stock is hot when adding as this will keep the temperature.

- Cook on low for 6–8 hours or if you want a faster meal, turn to high for 4–5 hours.

- Liquidise to a puree, adding more liquid if required.

- Serve with a drizzle with chilli oil for an extra kick.

Healthy tip: You may already know that chillies help speed up the metabolism but did you know they also have an anti-inflammatory effect?

Serves 4–6

Celery and Stilton Soup

I love this soup, it has a nice creamy texture and is not too cheesy. My son loves it too, though I have to keep the stilton a secret – if he saw me put it in he wouldn't eat it. The blue cheese is quite salty so you don't need to add any more to this.

Ingredients:
1 white onion, finely chopped
25g butter
1 bulb of celery, finely diced
1 large potato, finely diced
700ml hot water or hot vegetable stock (low salt as cheese is very salty)
150g blue cheese
Season to taste

- Remember to cut the vegetables into equal size so you get a more even cook.

- Add all ingredients apart from the stilton/blue cheese. Make sure the stock is hot when adding as this will keep the temperature.

- Cook on low for 6–7 hours or if you want a faster meal, turn to high for 3–4 hours.

- 10 minutes before serving, add the crumbled stilton. Allow to melt before liquidising gently. If you like a creamier soup, you can add a dollop or two of low fat creme fraiche or thick Greek yoghurt, though personally I don't think it needs this.

- Serve immediately or remove and leave to one side until needed. It does freeze well or keeps in an airtight container in the fridge for 2–3 days.

Healthy swap: I don't like things too salty so I use water instead of stock, but feel free to make the choice.

Hot Chilli, Vegetable and Bean Soup

Ingredients:
1 large red onion, diced
2 peppers, one of each colour, diced
1–2 chillies (or to taste), diced
3 cloves of garlic, roughly chopped
1 tin chopped tomatoes
2 sweet potatoes, diced
1 carrot, diced
2 sticks of celery, diced
1 tin mixed beans, drained
½ tsp cumin
2 tsp smoked paprika
1 tbsp tomato puree
500ml hot water or low salt vegetable

I love hot spicy food and this recipe combines the heat with wholesome vegetables and beans. Remember to chop everything in equal size – I like small diced vegetables in this. I love the flavour of smoked paprika, but if you prefer, you can use standard paprika.

- Cut the vegetables into equal size so you get a more even cook.

- Add all ingredients. Make sure the stock is hot when adding as this will keep the temperature.

- Cook on low for 6–8 hours or if you want a faster meal, turn to high for 4–5 hours.

- Serve with crusty bread and hummus for a delicious and filling meal.

Healthy tip: You can use water in this recipe instead of stock and it will still taste delicious! Season with black pepper.

Serves 4–6

Chicken and Vegetable Soup

The ultimate comfort soup when you are feeling under par. When you prepare the vegetables, dice them in equal size.

- Cut the vegetables into equal size so you get a more even cook.

- Add all ingredients. Make sure the stock is hot when adding as this will keep the temperature.

- Cook on low for 6–8 hours or if you want a faster meal, turn to high for 4–5 hours.

- Serve and garnish with freshly chopped parsley.

Healthy tip: If you have flu or a cold, add some chopped chilli and ginger. If you want a healthier soup, swap the chicken for turkey as it is lower fat.

Ingredients:
2 leeks, diced
2 cloves of garlic, roughly chopped.
2 sticks of celery, diced
2 carrots, diced
1–2 sweet potatoes, peeled and diced
1 white potato, peeled and diced
1 tin haricot beans, drained
½ tsp dried thyme
½ tsp dried parsley
700ml low salt chicken stock
300g boneless, skinless chicken, diced (thigh or breast)
freshly chopped parsley to garnish
Black pepper

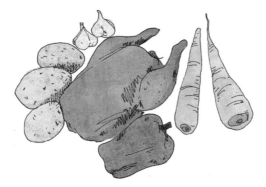

Serves 4–6

Beetroot and Tomato Soup

Ingredients:
450g beetroot, diced
1 large potato, diced
400g tomatoes, diced
1 red onion, diced
1 tsp caraway seeds
450ml hot low salt vegetable
    stock
Black pepper
3-4 tbsp low fat creme
    fraiche or 0% fat natural
    Greek yoghurt

What a fabulous colour! This recipe is for a hot soup. Add a swirl of natural yoghurt to serve.

- Remember to cut the vegetables into equal size so you get a more even cook.

- Add all ingredients apart from the creme fraiche/yoghurt. Make sure the stock is hot when adding as this will keep the temperature.

- Cook on low for 6–8 hours or if you want a faster meal, turn to high for 4–5 hours.

- Use your stick blender and whizz until smooth. Season to taste.

- Stir in the creme fraiche/yoghurt if you want a creamy soup, or use this to add a swirl when serving.

Healthy tip: Beetroot is high in fibre, potassium, vitamins A, C and B6 as well as being a good source of magnesium and iron. Known as a blood purifier, it has also been shown to help reduce heart disease, strokes and high blood pressure.

Serves 4

Broccoli and Stilton Soup

The slow cooker does not like dairy products being cooked for a long time, so you add the stilton in the last half hour of cooking.

Ingredients:
1 onion, finely chopped
1 stick of celery, chopped
1 head of broccoli, chopped
1 potato, diced
500-700ml low salt vegetable
  stock (depending on how
  thick you want the soup)
Black pepper
120g stilton or blue cheese

- Add all ingredients apart from the stilton. Make sure the stock is hot when adding as this will keep the temperature.

- Turn your slow cooker to low for 5–6 hours or if you want a faster meal, turn to high for 2–3 hours.

- 30 minutes before serving, stir in the crumbled stilton and season to taste. If you like a very creamy soup, you could add a couple of tbsp of 0% fat Greek yoghurt.

- Whizz with your stick blender until smooth. Serve with warm crusty bread.

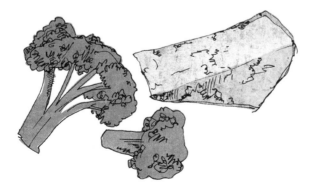

Cream of Celeriac Soup

Ingredients:
1 onion, finely chopped
2 cloves of garlic, roughly
chopped
1 leek, sliced
1 large potato, diced
750g celeriac, diced
700ml low salt vegetable
stock
1 bay leaf
Seasoning to taste
3 tbsp low fat creme fraiche
or 0% fat Greek yoghurt

Celeriac is contains antioxidants but it is also packed with Vitamin K, phosphorus, iron, manganese and copper.

- Remember to cut the vegetables into equal size so you get a more even cook.

- Add all ingredients apart from the creme fraiche/yoghurt. Make sure the stock is hot when adding as this will keep the temperature.

- Turn your slow cooker to low for 6–8 hours or if you want a faster meal, turn to high for 4–5 hours.

- Remove the bay leaf.

- Use your stick blender and whizz until smooth. Stir in the creme fraiche or yoghurt and season to taste.

- Serve immediately.

Serves 4–6

Rich Tomato Soup

I love tomato soup – if you like a bit of a kick, add some chilli flakes. For a creamy soup, stir in a couple of tablespoons of 0% fat Greek yoghurt before serving.

- Remember to cut the vegetables into equal size so you get a more even cook.

- Add all ingredients. Make sure the stock is hot when adding as this will keep the temperature.

- Turn your slow cooker to low for 6–8 hours or if you want a faster meal, turn to high for 4–5 hours.

- Whizz with a hand blender before serving.

- If you want a creamier soup you can stir in some Greek yoghurt or use this to form a swirl when serving.

Healthy tip: Tomatoes are rich in lycopene. According to the World Cancer Research Fund and the American Institute for Cancer Research report, lycopene probably reduces the risk of prostate cancer.

Ingredients:
1 red onion, diced
1–2 cloves of garlic, crushed
1 stick of celery, diced
1 carrot, diced
750g tomatoes, diced (can remove skins if you prefer)
100g sundried tomatoes (in oil), drained
2 tsp tomato puree
1 tsp paprika
2 bay leaves
1 tsp sugar
300–450ml low salt vegetable stock

Minestrone Soup

Ingredients:
1 red onion, chopped
1–2 cloves garlic, crushed
1 carrot, diced
1 red pepper, finely chopped
2 celery sticks, finely chopped
3–4 fresh tomatoes, peeled
    and chopped
1 tin red kidney beans,
    drained
50g fresh green beans,
    chopped
500mls low salt vegetable
    stock
3 tsp tomato puree
½ tsp of Cayenne pepper
1 tsp paprika
2 bay leaves
Season to taste
50g cabbage, shredded
50g dried spaghetti, broken
    into pieces
Small handful of basil (or to
    taste)

A lovely wholesome soup. When preparing this, try to keep the vegetables to a similar size – not only do they cook more evenly, they also look much better when you serve.

- Add all ingredients except the cabbage, spaghetti and basil. Make sure the stock is hot when adding as this will keep the temperature.

- Turn your slow cooker to low for 6–8 hours or if you want a faster meal, turn to high for 4–5 hours.

- 20 minutes before serving add shredded cabbage, dried spaghetti (broken into smaller pieces) and basil.

- Serve with crusty bread and hummus for a hearty meal.

- **Slow Cook Soups**

Serves 4

Carrot and Courgette Soup

Lovely flavours in this soup. As with all chunky soups, try to cut the vegetables into equal size for a more even cook as well as looking nicer when you serve.

Ingredients:
1 red onion, diced
2–3 carrots, diced
1–2 sweet potatoes, peeled and diced
3 courgettes, diced
3cm knuckle of fresh ginger, roughly chopped
500ml low salt vegetable stock
1 tsp dried thyme
Freshly chopped parsley to garnish

- Add all ingredients. Make sure the stock is hot when adding as this will keep the temperature.

- Turn your slow cooker to low for 8 hours or if you want a faster meal, turn to high for 4–5 hours.

- Serve with freshly chopped parsley garnish.

Healthy tip: Courgettes are high in beta carotene, a great source of folate. Be aware that they can absorb a lot of fat so if you are cooking them as a side vegetable with a main meal, try to avoid drowning them in butter or oil.

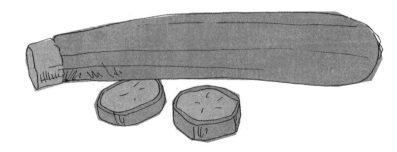

Slow Cook Soups

33

Serves 4

Nettle Soup

Ingredients:
1 large onion, diced
1 clove garlic, roughly
   chopped
1 potato, peeled and diced
2 sticks of celery, diced
500g young organic nettles
   (wear gloves when picking)
450ml low salt vegetable
   stock
2 tbsp low fat creme fraiche
   or 0% fat Greek yoghurt
Black pepper to taste

Nettles are rich in iron, calcium and really high in vitamin A. Made as a tea, they can help with urinary infections (the nettles act as a diuretic) and have been shown to help protect against kidney stones.

- Wash and chop nettles thoroughly (you may want to wear gloves for this). They will start to wilt if you run them under hot water, making it easier to pop into the slow cooker later.

- Add all ingredients apart for the creme fraiche or yoghurt. Make sure the stock is hot when adding as this will keep the temperature.

- Turn your slow cooker to cook on low for 4–6 hours.

- Cool slightly. Use electric hand blender to puree. Add the creme fraiche or yoghurt. Season to taste before serving.

Serves 4–6

Scotch Broth

This is my version of the classic. Keep the vegetables roughly the same size – thickly diced is best. This can be a really wholesome broth. I add some red lentils as I like their texture in the soup along with the barley.

- Chop the vegetables, making sure they are all roughly the same size as this helps an even cook and makes it look more presentable.

- Place everything in the slow cooker. Season to taste.

- Cook for 8 hours on high.

- Remove the bay leaf before serving.

Ingredients:
1 onion, diced
2–3 cloves of garlic, roughly chopped
2 carrots, diced
2 sweet potatoes, peeled and diced
½ turnip, diced
2 sticks of celery, diced
70g red lentils
70g pearl barley
750ml vegetable stock
1 bay leaf
Seasoning to taste

Poultry

Chicken is a good source of protein, as well as niacin and selenium. It also contains vitamin B6 and phosphorus. Dark chicken meat contains more zinc and B vitamins than white chicken meat but it also contain much more fat, so if you are watching your weight you are better to stick with the leaner white chicken meat and remember to remove all visible fat and skin as this really does pile on the calories.

Turkey contains less fat than chicken so you may want to consider switching if you are dieting. Turkey mince is also a great substitute for beef mince as it contains much less saturated fat. Turkey is rich in protein and selenium but is roughly two thirds lower in fat than chicken – but remember much depends on how you cook it. Turkey contains carnosine, which has been show to help to slow down ageing. As with chicken, the darker meat is higher in fat, so avoid this if you are watching your weight.

I prefer to buy free range or organic meat. A lot of supermarkets are now offering this at much cheaper prices and you will be surprised how much nicer it tastes.

Remember the rules when handling raw chicken – always clean the utensils and chopping boards thoroughly to avoid the spread of bacterial. Never cook frozen chicken – always make sure it is thoroughly defrosted, ideally in a fridge. Always make sure the chicken is thoroughly cooked before eating.

Always remember to thaw any frozen meat, poultry or fish before adding to the slow cooker.

Note: For all of the recipes in this chapter, **if your slow cooker needs to be preheated, turn it on 15 minutes before using.** Refer to your manufacturer's instructions for more information on your specific model temperatures.

Serves 4

Simple Coq Au Vin

A quick and easy variation of the traditional French favourite. Try using chicken thighs as they give a much nicer flavour in this dish.

- Prepare the vegetables and cut the chicken into large pieces.

- Place the coconut or olive oil in sauté pan.

- In a bowl, mix the flour, paprika and black pepper.

- Dip the chicken into the flour before adding to the hot, oiled sauté pan. Add the lardons and cook a little until it starts to brown. Remove from heat.

- Add all ingredients to the stock pot. Make sure the stock is hot when adding as this will keep the temperature.

- Cook for 8 hours on low or if you want a faster meal, turn to high for 5–6 hours.

- If the sauce is too liquid, mix 1–2 tbsp of cornflour with a little water. Pour this into the stock pot and turn the setting to high for 30 minutes. Remove the bay leaves before serving.

- Serve with sauté or mashed potatoes and green vegetables.

Ingredients:
Olive or coconut oil
500g chicken
2 tbsp flour
1 tsp paprika
Black pepper
12 shallots, whole
3-4 cloves of garlic, thickly
    sliced
200g smoked lardons
80g button mushrooms,
    halved or quartered
150ml red wine
150ml port
300ml chicken stock
2 bay leaves
2-3 sprigs of thyme
Seasoning

Allow 15 minutes to preheat your slow cooker.

Serves 4

Simple Chicken Curry

Ingredients:
1-3cm knuckle of fresh
  ginger, peeled
3-4 cloves of garlic
1-2 tbsp olive oil
Small handful coriander leaves
1 tbsp garam masala
6 tomatoes, chopped
3 chicken breasts, diced
1 large onion, chopped
1 pepper, sliced
1-2 sweet potatoes, diced
1-3 chillies, depending on
  personal taste and strength
1 stick of lemon grass, peeled
50g red lentils
200ml low fat coconut milk
3 tbsp 0% fat Greek yoghurt
Zest of a lime
Chopped coriander

Allow 15 minutes to preheat
your slow cooker.

You can't beat a good, homemade curry. Forget the high fat, high salt jars of sauce, this recipe uses your own homemade paste. Simply store in the fridge in an airtight container or freeze until needed.

- In a food processor, add the ginger, garlic, chilli, olive oil, coriander, garam masala and tomatoes. Whizz until you form a paste. Leave to one side to rest. (Store in the fridge or freeze until needed.)

- Remember to cut the vegetables and chicken into equal size so you get a more even cook. Remove the skin and any visible fat from the chicken breasts.

- Place all the ingredients into the slow cooker apart from the Greek yoghurt and lime. If the curry is too thick, add a little water.

- Cook on low for 6–8 hours or if you want a faster meal, turn to high for 3–4 hours.

- 20–30 minutes before serving, stir in the Greek yoghurt, chopped coriander and the zest of a lime.

- Stir and serve on a bed of rice – ideally brown rice or basmati if you are health conscious.

Healthy swap: This recipe uses chicken, but you can also use lean turkey breast or why not add to some wholesome veggies? I have used low-fat coconut milk in this recipe. If you can't find low fat, avoid adding full fat coconut milk as it is very calorific. Instead add more yoghurt.

Poultry

Serves 4–6

Hearty Chicken Casserole

This is a great standby to use up any leftovers, whether it is chicken or some vegetables that need using up.

- Add all ingredients. Make sure the stock is hot when adding as this will keep the temperature.

- Turn your slow cooker to low and cook for 6–8 hours, or if you want a faster meal, turn to high for 4–5 hours.

- Serve with mini jacket potatoes.

Healthy tip: Adding red lentils to this casserole adds to the nutritional value as well as helping to thicken the stock. You could swap the red lentils for a dried soup mix.

Ingredients:
1 red onion, finely chopped
1–2 cloves of garlic, crushed
2 sticks of celery, chopped
1 large leek, chopped
1 large carrot, diced
1 large potato, peeled and diced
1 large sweet potato, peeled and diced
1 tin tomatoes (or 4–6 ripe fresh tomatoes)
400g chicken pieces (thigh, legs or breast)
100g lardons (optional)
75g red lentils
700ml chicken stock
2 tsp paprika
1 bay leaf

Allow 15 minutes to preheat your slow cooker.

Serves 4

Chicken with Creamy Mushroom and Port Sauce

Ingredients:
4–6 chicken breasts, left whole or halved
2–3 cloves of garlic, crushed
1 red onion, diced
1 stick of celery, diced
120g mixed wild or chestnut mushrooms, halved
200ml port
300ml chicken stock
3 heaped tsp cornflour
1 tsp dried tarragon

Allow 15 minutes to preheat your slow cooker.

A lovely, easy meal to impress friends for a dinner party. If you don't have port, you can use red or white wine.

- Add all ingredients, apart from the cornflour to the slow cooker. Make sure the stock is hot when adding as this will keep the temperature.

- Mix the cornflour with a little water to form a liquid paste, add this to the stock pot and stir well.

- Turn your slow cooker to low and cook for 6–8 hours.

- Serve with green vegetables and mashed potato.

Poultry

Serves 4–6

Chicken, Bean and Sundried Tomato Casserole

A deliciously light casserole, the borlotti beans add additional protein and fibre.

- Add all ingredients. Make sure the stock is hot when adding as this will keep the temperature.

- Turn your slow cooker to low and cook for 6–8 hours.

- Serve with crusty wholemeal bread rolls and hummus.

Ingredients:
1 red onion, diced
2 cloves of garlic, crushed
3 chicken breasts, diced
1 tin borlotti beans, drained
1 red pepper, diced
2 sticks of celery, finely diced
1 tin chopped tomatoes
30g sundried tomatoes, drained of oil
1–2 tsp sundried tomato puree
100ml red wine
300ml chicken stock
1 tsp oregano
½ tsp thyme
1 tsp paprika
1 bay leaf

Allow 15 minutes to preheat your slow cooker.

Serves 4–6

Slow-cooked Whole Chicken and Vegetables

Ingredients:
One whole chicken
Coconut or olive oil
2–3 tsp paprika
2 red onions, roughly chopped
2 carrots, thickly sliced
1–2 leeks, thickly sliced
2 celery sticks, thickly sliced
150g lardons roughly chopped
 (optional)
2–3 bay leaves
1 tsp dried tarragon
700ml chicken stock
Seasoning to taste

Allow 15 minutes to preheat
your slow cooker.

Slow cooked whole chicken is incredibly tender and moist. Sounds obvious but make sure your chicken fits in your slow cooker.

- Heat the olive oil or coconut oil in a large sauté pan. Carefully brown the skin of the chicken. This will help give it a golden glow without having to resort to placing under a grill or in an oven before serving.

- Sprinkle the chicken with paprika.

- Place chicken in the slow cooker. Add all the vegetables and lardons, spreading them evenly around and over the chicken.

- Add the bay leaves, tarragon, seasoning and pour the hot chicken stock over the chicken.

- Cook on low for 6 hours.

- You can drain the chicken from the stock, or serve as it is. If you want to thicken the stock, remove the chicken ready to carve. Mix some cornflour with a little cold water and add to the stock. Place on high to thicken.

- Serve with roasted potatoes and green vegetables.

Poultry

Serves 4

Chicken in Red Wine Sauce

My mum used to make this when we were children and it was always a big favourite of ours. She served with it with mini roasts or sauté potatoes and vegetables. You can actually make a veggie version of this by supplementing the chicken fillets for Quorn fillets – cooking time will be halved for this.

- Add all ingredients apart from the cornflour. Make sure the stock is hot when adding as this will keep the temperature.

- Mix the cornflour with a little water and stir into the slow cooker.

- Turn your slow cooker to low and cook for 6–8 hours, or if you want a faster meal, turn to high for 4–5 hours.

- Serve with small roasts or sauté potatoes and vegetables.

Ingredients:
1 onion, chopped
2–3 cloves of garlic crushed
1 red pepper, diced
500g chicken (thigh, legs or breast)
2 tsp paprika
1 tin chopped tomatoes
200ml red wine
300ml chicken stock
150g button mushrooms, halved or left whole
1 tsp dried tarragon
Seasoning to taste
1 heaped tbsp cornflour

Allow 15 minutes to preheat your slow cooker.

Cajun Chicken Casserole

Ingredients:
1 onion, chopped
2–3 cloves of garlic, crushed
1 chilli, chopped finely
2–3 tsp Cajun spice
1 tsp paprika
Red pepper, sliced
400g chicken pieces (thigh, legs or breast)
2 sticks of celery, diced
1 tin chopped tomatoes

Allow 15 minutes to preheat your slow cooker.

Turn up the heat with this lovely Cajun casserole.

- Add all ingredients. Make sure the stock is hot when adding as this will keep the temperature.

- Turn your slow cooker to low and cook for 6–8 hours, or if you want a faster meal, turn to high for 4–5 hours.

Healthy swap: To cut down fat, remove any skin or fat from the chicken. If you want a lower fat dish, opt for turkey.

Serves 4–6

Chicken, Bean and Chorizo One Pot

Packed with flavour, this is a great dish when you want a tasty meal for friends. You can use chicken breast, thighs or drumsticks. This recipe uses thighs as they add more flavour but if I am making it for children, I tend to use chicken breasts.

- Place all the ingredients in the slow cooker – make sure the stock is hot when you add it. Combine well. Season to taste. Add more stock if needed.

- Cook on low for 6–8 hours.

- Serve with crusty bread.

Ingredients:
1 large red onion, diced
2 cloves of garlic, roughly
  chopped
1 tin chopped tomatoes
2 tins cannellini beans,
  drained
1 large sweet potato, diced
2–3 chorizo sausages, sliced
  (ideally skinless as the skin
  is tough)
4–6 chicken thighs
250ml low salt chicken stock
1 tsp tomato puree
Pinch of cayenne pepper
Pinch of smoked paprika
½ tsp dried parsley
2 heaped tsp cornflour (mixed
  in a little cold water)

Allow 15 minutes to preheat
your slow cooker.

Serves 4

Chicken Vindaloo

Ingredients:
2 tbsp olive oil
1 chilli
2 cloves of garlic
3-4 tbsp vindaloo paste
1 tsp turmeric
1 tsp ground cumin
2 tomatoes
250ml water or stock
Small handful coriander leaves
1 large onion, diced
500g chicken fillets, diced

Allow 15 minutes to preheat your slow cooker.

This is quite a hot dish, so adjust the spices to suit your own taste. I normally make several curry dishes, including a lentil dahl, and serve together, so you can have a selection of flavours and heat. If you double up the recipe, you can freeze what you don't use ready for another meal.

- Place all the ingredients apart from the onion and chicken in the food processor and whizz until you form a paste.

- If you are marinating the meat, place the chicken in a bowl or freezer bag, pour on the paste and marinate for a few hours. Skip this step if you don't want to marinate.

- Put the chicken, paste and onion in the slow cooker. Combine well. Add more water if needed.

- Cook on high for 4–5 hours or low for 6 hours.

- Serve with rice and Indian chutneys.

Cooking tip: I like to marinate this for at least 2 hours before placing in the slow cooker. You don't have to do this, but I think it increases the flavour.

Healthy swap: Turkey has lower fat content than chicken. Cooked in the slow cooker it can be just a succulent as chicken.

Serves 4

Moroccan Style Chicken and Vegetable Tagine

I love using spices to create new dishes – this recipe uses a lot of spices, but allows them to infuse and the taste is amazing. If you don't like things too hot, you can omit the chilli.

- Chop the chicken into chunks. Place in a bowl.

- In a food processor add 2 tablespoons of olive oil, the spices, ginger, chilli, half the chopped herbs and the tomatoes. Whizz to form a marinade.

- Pour this onto the chicken and cover with clingfilm. Leave to marinate overnight or for at least 2 hours. When you are ready to cook, bring it back up to room temperature for at least 1 hour.

- Place a little olive oil in your sauté pan on a medium heat. Add the onion, garlic and pepper and cook for 3–5 minutes before adding the chicken, holding back most of the marinade until you add the remaining ingredients.

- Cook for 5 minutes before adding all the other ingredients, including the marinade.

- Simmer gently for 5 minutes before adding the remaining herbs and transfer into the slow cooker.

- Place on low and cook for 4–6 hours.

- Serve with couscous.

Ingredients:
Olive oil
3-4 chicken (thigh, legs or breast), diced
2.5cm knuckle of ginger, finely chopped
1 tsp paprika
1 tsp cumin
1 tsp turmeric
1 tsp cinnamon
Small handful of mint leaves
Small handful of coriander leaves
1 chilli, finely diced
1 large onion, sliced
2 cloves of garlic, roughly chopped
1 green pepper, thickly diced
2 sweet potatoes, peeled and cut into chunks
1 carrot, diced
60g green beans
1 tin chickpeas, drained
1 tin chopped tomatoes,
300-400ml chicken stock

Allow 15 minutes to preheat your slow cooker.

Herby Garlic and Lemon Chicken

Ingredients:

Olive oil or coconut oil

4 chicken fillets (breast or thighs work well)

1 onion, diced

2-4 cloves of garlic, roughly chopped

Juice and zest of 1 lemon

300ml chicken stock

½ tsp dried thyme

½ tsp dried marjoram

½ tsp dried parsley

Handful of fresh parsley

Allow 15 minutes to preheat your slow cooker.

A really easy recipe – the chicken is cooked in a lovely stock. Serve with new potatoes and green vegetables for a light and tasty dinner.

- In a sauté pan, add the olive or coconut oil. Cook the chicken for 3–5 minutes.

- Remove and place in the slow cooker.

- Add all the remaining ingredients into the slow cooker apart from the fresh parsley.

- Cook on high for 3 hours or low for 5–6 hours.

- Just before serving, stir in the fresh parsley.

- If you want a creamy sauce, you can stir in a few tablespoons of low fat creme fraiche.

- Serve with new minted potatoes and steamed green vegetables.

Pork

Although a good source of protein, pork is high in cholesterol and saturated fat so try to refrain from having too much if you just want to look after your health. However, like other red meats, it is a good source of protein, vitamin B12, iron and selenium. Remove any visible fat. It works well in the slow cooker creating a succulent, tender meat. Pork shouldn't be eaten pink or rare, check that there is no pink meat and the juices are no longer pink or red.

Be aware that pork products such as processed ham, bacon and sausages do vary in quality. Some hams and bacon contain lots of added water. Sausages can be made with very cheap ingredients so always read the labels and buy the best quality you can afford.

Note: For all of the recipes in this chapter, **if your slow cooker needs to be preheated, turn it on 15 minutes before using.** Refer to your manufacturer's instructions for more information on your specific model temperatures.

Serves 4

Slow Sweet and Sour Pork

Ingredients:
500g pork, cubed or strips
1 red onion, diced
3-4 cloves of garlic, crushed
1 yellow pepper, sliced
2-3cm knuckle of ginger, finely chopped
100ml white wine
75ml red wine vinegar
50g brown sugar
100ml water
150g pineapple chunks and natural juice
3-4 tbsp soy sauce
2 tbsp tomato ketchup

Allow 15 minutes to preheat your slow cooker.

You don't have to use pork for this dish, you could opt for chicken or turkey for lower fat options. Opt for basmati or brown rice to help balance the meal.

- You can brown the pork off if you prefer, before placing it into the slow cooker, but I take the easy route and just add all the ingredients to the slow cooker.

- Stir well to ensure it is evenly distributed. Place the slow cooker on low and cook for 8 hours.

- Once cooked, if you prefer a thicker sauce, add 2 teaspoons of cornflour, mixed with 50ml of water, combine well and then add to the pork mix. Turn the slow cooker to high and cook for 30 minutes.

- Serve on a bed of rice.

Serves 6–8

Slow-cooked Gammon

My mum is a big fan of gammon and likes to cook this on special
occasions.

- Place the gammon in the slow cooker.

- Pour in the apple juice or water.

- Add nutmeg, cinnamon, ginger and orange. Season to taste.

- Cook the gammon on a low heat for 8–10 hours or high for
  6–7 hours.

- The gammon will have a thick skin on it which can be
  removed before slicing or follow as below.

- If you want this to look nicer (the skin can make it look a bit
  unappetising), you can use a sharp knife and score the skin in
  a diamond pattern. Place cloves in the diamonds created.
  Brush with honey and place in a conventional oven set at
  190°C until golden and crisp.

- Delicious sliced and served with parsley sauce and sauté
  potatoes.

Ingredients:
1 gammon joint
1 litre of apple juice or water
2–3 sticks of cinnamon
1 tsp nutmeg
2–3cm knuckle of ginger,
   roughly chopped
1 orange, quartered
Seasoning to taste

Allow 15 minutes to preheat
your slow cooker.

Cowboy Baked Beans

Ingredients:
½ tsp coconut oil (or olive oil)
1 red onion, diced
1 pack of back bacon, diced
  (all fat removed)
2 cloves of garlic, roughly
  chopped
75g chorizo sausage, sliced
  (skin removed)
2 tins haricot beans, drained
100ml apple juice
1 tin chopped tomatoes
1 tbsp tomato puree
Dash of Worcestershire sauce
1 tsp wholegrain mustard
½ tsp cumin
½ tsp chilli powder
1–2 tsp smoked paprika
  (optional)

Allow 15 minutes to preheat
your slow cooker.

Forget tinned beans, make this dish to impress – it is really tasty. If you fancy a smoky flavour, add a teaspoon or two of smoked paprika.

- Place the coconut oil in a sauté pan. Add the onion, garlic, bacon and chorizo and cook until it starts to soften and bacon starts to brown. Place in the slow cooker.

- Add all ingredients and combine well. Add more liquid (either water or apple juice) if needed.

- Turn your slow cooker to low and cook gently for 6–8 hours.

- Serve the beans on their own or as an accompaniment in the same way as you use baked beans.

- Store any leftovers in the fridge until needed.

Pork

Serves 4–6

Pork Tenderloin

Serve with roast potatoes, green vegetables and a spoonful of spicy apple sauce – see Chapter 13, Preserves, Chutneys and Sauces.

- Place the tenderloin in the slow cooker. Add the onion and garlic.

- Mix the sugar, wholegrain mustard, soy sauce, wine and stock together and pour onto the tenderloin.

- Cook on low for 4–5 hours.

- Drain and slice, ready to serve with the roast potatoes, green vegetables and apple sauce.

Ingredients:
1kg pork tenderloin
1 red onion, finely chopped
2–3 cloves of garlic, crushed
1 tsp sugar
2 tsp wholegrain mustard
3 tsp soy sauce
200ml red wine
200ml low salt stock

Allow 15 minutes to preheat your slow cooker.

Serves 4–6

Chorizo, Vegetable and Chickpea Casserole

If you like smoked paprika flavours, you will love this casserole. Combining chorizo with vegetables and fresh green cabbage is delicious. Serve with bread for a filling lunch.

Ingredients:
Olive oil or coconut oil
1 red onion, diced
2–3 cloves of garlic, roughly
    chopped (optional)
4–6 chorizo sausages, diced
400g new potatoes, halved
2 sweet potatoes, peeled and
    diced
1 tin chickpeas, drained
1 bay leaf
500ml low salt chicken or
    vegetable stock
Half a savoy cabbage (or dark
    greens) shredded

Allow 15 minutes to preheat
your slow cooker.

- Heat a very small amount of olive or coconut oil in a sauté pan.

- Add the onion, garlic and chorizo and cook until the sausage starts to release the oils.

- Place this in the slow cooker and add all the remaining ingredients apart from the cabbage. Combine well and season to taste.

- Place on low and cook for 6–8 hours.

- 20 minutes before you are ready to serve, add the cabbage.

- Serve with homemade bread and hummus for a delicious lunch.

- Pork

Serves 4

Pork Goulash

This recipe is based on the traditional Hungarian stew.

- Place the olive oil or coconut oil in your sauté pan, heat the oil and cook the onion, garlic and pork until browned and the onions start to soften. You can ignore this part if you don't want to brown the meat.

- Place this in the slow cooker and add all remaining ingredients apart from the creme fraiche and parsley. Cook on high for 4 hours, or low for 6 hours.

- Prior to serving add the remaining chopped parsley and stir in the creme fraiche (you can use natural yoghurt, I find that Total Greek Yoghurt is the best).

Ingredients:
Olive or coconut oil
1 red onion, finely sliced
1-2 cloves of garlic, crushed
2 red peppers, finely sliced
500g pork, cut into chunks
3-4 tsp smoked paprika
1 tin chopped tomatoes
1-2 tsp tomato puree
200 ml red wine
200 ml beef stock
Handful of freshly chopped
    parsley
150 ml creme fraiche

Allow 15 minutes to preheat
your slow cooker.

Serves 4–6

Cider and Apple Pork Fillet

Ingredients:
1 pork fillet (roughly 500g)
1 large red onion, diced
2 cloves of garlic, roughly
   chopped (optional)
2–3 apples, cut into thick
   wedges (not peeled)
200ml cider
250ml stock

Allow 15 minutes to preheat
your slow cooker.

The slow-cooked pork simply melts in the mouth – the cider and apple works really well with the pork.

- Place the fillet in the slow cooker. Add the onion and garlic.

- Heat the stock and mix with the cider.

- Pour onto the fillet. Add the apples and season to taste.

- Cook for 5–6 hours.

- Serve sliced with mash and green vegetables.

Pork

Serves 4–8

Ham Hock

This is a really cheap, tasty ham. You should be able to fit 3–4 hocks in your slow cooker, depending on the size of the cooker. I use water to cook the ham in as I have found stock creates a very salty ham. One ham hock should feed two people. Slow cooked, the outer skin does stay white. You can cut this off, or if you like it crispy/baked, you can place in your conventional oven for 30 minutes. Flake off the ham to use hot or cold. Perfect for sandwiches, filling for a quiche, soups, or simply on its own with egg and chips or a salad. One of my favourites is ham with a parsley sauce, sauté potatoes and green vegetables.

Ingredients:
2–4 ham hocks
1 onion, quartered
1 carrot, roughly chopped
Water

Allow 15 minutes to preheat your slow cooker.

- Place the onion, carrot and ham hocks in the slow cooker. Fill with water until the ham is just covered.

- Cook on low for 6–8 hours.

- Remove the hocks. Cut away the skin and slice or flake the ham away from the bone. Use as you wish, hot or cold.

- If you like a baked hock, glaze with some honey – you can stud with some cloves if you prefer. Place in the oven at 190°C and cook for 30 minutes or until golden.

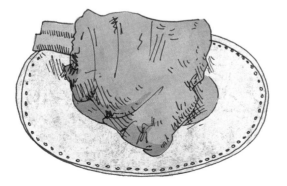

Serves 4–6

Slow Roasted Pork with Rosemary and Mustard

Ingredients:
Loin or leg of pork, rolled and
  tied
Olive oil or coconut oil
2 tbsp chopped rosemary
2 tbsp wholegrain mustard
2 tbsp dried oregano
750ml water

Allow 15 minutes to preheat
your slow cooker.

Use loin or leg of pork in this recipe. You can use shoulder but increase the cooking time by 1 hour for this.

- Mix all the herbs, oil and mustard together in a bowl and spread this over the joint.

- Place a little olive oil or coconut oil in a sauté pan and brown the joint, sealing it all around.

- Pour the warm water in the slow cooker.

- Place the joint in the slow cooker.

- Cook on high for 5 hours.

- If you want a joint that is more browned, you can remove from the slow cooker and place in a conventional oven until browned, but once sliced, this meat is lovely and tender with a great flavour so you don't want to dry it out too much.

- Serve with roast potatoes and green vegetables.

Lamb

Lamb and beef work so well in the slow cooker – they really benefit from a long slow cook. If you prefer a stew or casserole, choose cheaper cuts such as neck fillet, boneless loin, brisket, shanks or even shoulder. Cooked slowly they can produce flavoursome and tender meats.

Lamb is a good source of protein, but like other red meats is very high in saturated fat and cholesterol. It is high in protein, iron, zinc, vitamin B12 and amino acid carnitine as well as containing vitamin B6, pantothenic acid, phosphorus and manganese, vitamin A, riboflavin, niacin, copper and selenium.

Note: For all of the recipes in this chapter, **if your slow cooker needs to be preheated, turn it on 15 minutes before using.** Refer to your manufacturer's instructions for more information on your specific model temperatures.

Serves 4–6

Irish Lamb Stew

Ingredients:
1 onion, finely chopped
2 cloves of garlic, crushed
2 carrots, thickly sliced
1 sweet potato, diced
2–3 potatoes, thickly diced
500g lamb
150g bacon or lardons
½ tsp dried thyme
1 tsp dried parsley
1 bay leaf
600ml lamb stock

Allow 15 minutes to preheat your slow cooker.

A hearty recipe. This recipe can be doubled up to make Lamb Hotpot – see Chapter 11, Two for One page 126.

2 for 1

- Add all ingredients.

- Make sure the stock is hot when adding as this will keep the temperature.

- Turn your slow cooker to low and cook for for 8–10 hours.

- Serve with a garnish of freshly chopped parsley.

Healthy swap: You could add a handful of dried soup mix to add more nutrients.

● Lamb

Serves 4

Slow-cooked Lamb, Vegetable and Olive Tagine

Speak to your butcher for advice on the best cut of lamb for the slow cooker. This is a lovely warming dish, with a bit of a kick. Serve with rice or couscous.

- Prepare the vegetables and remove all visible fat from the meat.

- Place some olive oil or coconut oil in a large sauté pan and heat gently on a hob.

- Add the onions, garlic, ginger and chilli and cook until starting to soften. Add the spices and cook for 1–2 minutes to allow the flavours out.

- Add the meat and brown well in the spices.

- Transfer back to slow cook and add all remaining ingredients apart from the fresh coriander and the almonds.

- Place on low setting and cook for 8–10 hours – the longer, the more tender the meat.

- Add a sprinkle of fresh coriander leaves and flaked almonds before serving.

Healthy swap: Remove all visible fat from the meat. Swap the olive oil for coconut oil.

Ingredients:
Olive oil
1 large red onion, finely chopped
3 cloves of garlic, crushed
2 tsp ground cumin
1 tsp ground coriander
1–2 chopped chillies
1 tsp turmeric
2 inch knuckle of ginger
500g lamb stewing meat, cut into chunks
2 sweet potatoes, peeled and diced
1–2 carrots, diced
1 yellow pepper, diced
600ml low salt lamb stock
200g pitted olives
Fresh coriander leaves
Flaked almonds

Allow 15 minutes to preheat your slow cooker.

Lamb Shanks

Ingredients:
2 red onions, sliced
3 cloves of garlic, crushed
2 sticks of celery, finely sliced
1 leek, finely sliced
1 carrot, finely diced
1 sweet potato
4 lamb shanks
1 tin chopped tomatoes
300ml red wine
3 tsp balsamic vinegar
400ml low salt lamb stock, hot
1 bay leaf
Sprigs of fresh thyme and
    rosemary

Allow 15 minutes to preheat
your slow cooker.

One of my dad's favourite dishes. This really benefits from a slow cook –
you want the lamb to fall of the bone.

- Prepare all the vegetables, making sure they are roughly the same size so they cook evenly.

- Place all the ingredients in the slow cooker. Make sure they are combined well and evenly distributed.

- Set the slow cooker to low and cook for 8–10 hours, until the lamb is tender.

- Prior to serving, if your liquid is too thin, stir in 1–2 teaspoons of cornflour, dissolved in a little water, turn heat up to thicken for 5–10 minutes.

- Season to taste before serving.

Healthy swap: You can opt for a low calorie red wine if you want to reduce the calorie intake.

Serves 4–6

Slow-cooked Leg of Lamb

This is a really simple dish and makes the most tender lamb. You can coat with whatever herbs and spices you wish. If you buy the leg of lamb and it does not fit in your slow cooker, you can either saw off the end of the bone (your butcher can do this), or buy without the bone.

Ingredients:
Leg of lamb
3–5 cloves of garlic
1 tsp rosemary
Juice of 1 lemon
Salt
Black pepper
1 tbsp honey
300ml red wine

Allow 15 minutes to preheat your slow cooker.

- Combine the garlic, rosemary, lemon, salt, pepper and honey together to form a paste. Rub this into the leg of lamb. Cover and place in the fridge overnight.

- Place the lamb in the slow cooker. Add 300ml of red wine around the sides of the lamb.

- Set to low and cook for 8 hours.

Healthy tip: You can buy low calorie red wine in supermarkets.

Lamb •

63

Serves 4

Lamb Moussaka

Ingredients:

1 onion, diced
2 cloves garlic, crushed
400g lean lamb mince
1 tin chopped tomatoes
2 tsp tomato puree
2 tsp cinnamon powder
1 tsp dried mint
2–3 aubergines, sliced
300ml low fat creme fraiche
    or 0% fat-free Greek
    yoghurt
2 eggs, beaten
50g mature cheddar or
    parmesan cheese
Seasoning

Allow 15 minutes to preheat
your slow cooker.

You may not have thought about cooking a moussaka in the slow cooker but it does make the meat tender, though please drain the fat from the meat before placing in the slow cooker or you will be in danger of a very fatty dish.

- In a sauté pan, cook onion and garlic in a little olive or coconut oil. Add lamb mince and cook until brown. Drain away any excess fat.

- Add tomatoes and puree, mint and cinnamon and cook for another 2–3 minutes.

- Spray the inside of the stock pot with olive oil to help prevent the moussaka from sticking.

- Place layer of mince in slow cooker, followed by a layer of aubergine. Finish with layer of mince.

- Place on low and cook for 4–6 hours, or high for 3–4 hours.

- 1 hour before serving, mix the creme fraiche or yoghurt with the eggs and grated cheese. Season with black pepper and pour over the final layer of mince. Garnish with a sprinkle of parmesan and cook for another hour.

- If you want a golden top, place under a grill for 5–10 minutes before serving.

- Serve with a lovely green salad.

Healthy swap: You can use low-fat mature cheddar for this recipe or opt for some nutritional yeast flakes – this gives you the cheesy flavour without the additional fat content – it is also packed with B vitamins.

Serves 4–6

Lamb, Shallot and Mushroom Casserole

Remember to cut the vegetables into equal size so you get a more even cook.

- Add all ingredients. Make sure the stock is hot when adding as this will keep the temperature.

- Turn your slow cooker to low and cook for 6–8 hours.

Healthy tip: You can buy low calorie wine from supermarkets. Great to keep the calorie count lower.

Ingredients:
250g shallots or baby onions
2 cloves of garlic, crushed
500g lamb (chunks)
200g button mushrooms
1 tin chopped tomatoes
2 tsp tomato puree
200ml red wine
300ml lamb stock
1 tsp paprika
Sprigs of fresh rosemary
Season to taste

Allow 15 minutes to preheat your slow cooker.

Serves 4–6

Wholesome Lamb and Vegetable Casserole

Ingredients:

1 large onion, diced

2-3 carrots, diced

1-2 sweet potatoes, peeled and diced

3-4 potatoes, peeled and diced

75g dried soup mix

700g lamb, cut into chunks

800ml low salt chicken, lamb or vegetable stock

½ tsp dried parsley

1 bay leaf

Allow 15 minutes to preheat your slow cooker.

If you are not a fan of lamb, this recipe also works well with chicken – a thick broth liquid with lovely chunky vegetables and meat.

- Remember to chop your vegetables chunky and roughly to the same size so it cooks evenly.

- You can brown the meat if you prefer but I have cooked both browned and added straight to the stock pot and really can't tell any difference, so now I skip the browning (and the additional washing up) and add all the ingredients together – making sure the stock is hot when you add it.

- Place on low and cook for 8–10 hours.

Healthy tip: For added nutrition, the recipe includes dried soup mix. You can buy these in most supermarkets (you will find them with the other dried pulses and beans). They normally contain red lentils, split peas, dried peas, barley and aduki beans.

Serves 4

Tunisian Lamb

I was lucky enough to holiday in Tunisian island of Djerba last year and we had some amazing dishes. This is a very easy recipe, which gives you the flavour without too much work.

- Place the olive oil or coconut in the sauté pan and add the lamb. Brown off, drain and place in the slow cooker.

- Add all the remaining ingredients apart from the flaked almonds.

- Cook on low for 8–10 hours.

- Just before serving, stir in the flaked almonds.

- Serve with couscous.

Healthy tip: Dried apricots are a rich source of iron.

Ingredients:
Olive or coconut oil
500g lamb, diced
1 large onion, diced
1 large carrot, diced
1 sweet potato, peeled and diced
2–3cm knuckle of ginger, roughly chopped
2 cloves of garlic, roughly chopped
2–4 tbsp harissa paste (depending on strength)
1 tsp ground cinnamon
8 olives, halved
8–12 apricots
500ml lamb stock
50g flaked almonds

Allow 15 minutes to preheat your slow cooker.

Beef

Beef works really well in the slow cooker, but remember it is high in saturated fat so limit your red meat consumption. It is a rich source of protein and B vitamins, particularly vitamin B12, as well as being quite a good source of zinc, iron, phosphorus and copper.

Mince is great for a number of meals – bolognaise, shepherd's pie or even a chilli. Opt for lean mince. You can cook the mince and drain any fat before adding to your dish to avoid extra fat content in your meal.

If making a stew or casserole, choose cheaper cuts. Feather steak, brisket, oxtail, diced steak, shin and leg are all perfect for slow cooking. Cooked slowly they can produce flavoursome and tender meats.

Note: For all of the recipes in this chapter, **if your slow cooker needs to be preheated, turn it on 15 minutes before using.** Refer to your manufacturer's instructions for more information on your specific model temperatures.

Serves 4–6

Spicy Beef and Bean Casserole

Packed with protein and fibre – this is a little bit like a chunky chilli. Serve with rice or mashed potato.

- Mix the flour and ground ginger together and season. Dip the beef chunks into the flour ensuring it is evenly covered.

- If you would like to brown the meat, you can do so on a sauté pan or if you slow cooker is hob proof, add some olive or coconut oil, onion and garlic and brown the beef. This is not necessary, so feel free to avoid this step.

- Place all the ingredients in the slow cooker, ensuring they are evenly distributed.

- Cover and cook slowly for 6–8 hours.

- Serve with rice or mashed potatoes and steam vegetables.

Ingredients:
1–2 tbsp plain flour
1 tsp ground ginger
400g stewing beef
Seasoning
1 red onion, diced
2 cloves of garlic, chopped
1 chilli, finely chopped
1 red pepper, sliced
1 tin tomatoes
2 carrots, sliced
1 sweet potato, sliced
1 tin red kidney beans, drained
1 tin mixed beans, drained
1–2 tsp chilli powder (depending on personal taste)
1 tbsp Worcester sauce
50ml red wine vinegar
300ml beef stock

Allow 15 minutes to preheat your slow cooker.

Serves 4–6

Beef, Vegetable and Barley Casserole

Ingredients:
1 red onion, diced
300g beef steak, diced
2 sticks of celery, diced
2 carrots, diced
1 sweet potato, diced
1 leeks, diced
1 tin chopped tomatoes
75g pearl barley
50g red lentils
1 litre low salt or homemade
   beef stock
1 tsp paprika
1 tsp thyme
Black pepper
Small handful of freshly
   chopped parsley

Allow 15 minutes to preheat
your slow cooker.

Red onions, carrots and sweet potato contain powerful antioxidants. Pearl barley is full of soluble fibre beta-glucan – which has been show to help lower cholesterol and keep blood sugars stable. Rich in iron, potassium, immune boosting zinc, manganese and vitamin B3.

- Chop the vegetables and meat, removing all traces of fat from the beef. Rinse the pearl barley.

- Place all the ingredients in the stock pot apart from the chopped parsley. Place the root vegetables nearer the base as these take longer to cook. Make sure the beef stock is hot before adding – make sure the meat and vegetables are covered well. You may not need to use all the stock.

- Turn your slow cooker to auto for 8–10 hours. If you don't have an auto button, turn to low for 8–10 hours. I would not recommend using the high setting to speed things up as this dish, especially if using cheaper cuts of meat, benefits from a long slow cook.

- Check the dish 30 minutes before serving and add the chopped parsley. Season with black pepper to taste (you don't need to add salt if you are health conscious!). If you feel the stock needs thickening, add 1–2 heaped teaspoons of cornflower mixed with a little water and cook on high for 30 minutes.

Serves 4–6

Beef and Cranberry Casserole

The cranberries and allspice give this dish a Christmassy feel.

- Prepare the beef into chunks. If not moist, wet with a little water. Mix the flour and allspice together. Dip the beef into the flour mix to ensure it is evenly coated.

- Heat the coconut or olive oil in your sauté pan and cook the onion, garlic and beef until browned and the onions start to soften. Drain any excess fat.

- Place this in the slow cooker and add all remaining ingredients. Cook on low for 8–10 hours.

- Season before serving.

Ingredients:
500g stewing beef
1–2 tbsp flour
2 tsp allspice
Olive or coconut oil
1 onion, finely chopped
2–3 cloves of garlic, finely chopped
2 sticks of celery, sliced
1 large carrot, diced
1 sweet potato, diced
200g cranberries (fresh or frozen)
1 orange, zest and juice
200ml red wine
400–500ml beef stock

Allow 15 minutes to preheat your slow cooker.

Serves 4–6

Beef and Ale Stew with Herb Dumplings

Ingredients:
Plain flour
2–3 tsp paprika
Beef stewing steak, chunks
1 red onion, finely chopped
1 tbsp red currant jelly
1 leek, finely sliced
2–3 carrots, sliced
1 parsnip, sliced
125g button mushrooms
600ml ale
1 beef stock cube (I use Knorr
    Beef Stock Pot Gel)
1 bay leaf

Dumpling ingredients
100g self-raising flour
50g suet
2–3 tsp mixed herbs
4 tbsp water

Allow 15 minutes to preheat
your slow cooker.

This is a very traditional recipe but that doesn't mean we can't give it a healthy twist. With a few tweaks we can make a wholesome dish that will satisfy most appetites. This recipe can be doubled up to make Beef and Ale Pies – see Chapter 11, Two for One. Remember if you are doubling up this recipe, you will need to remove half before adding the dumplings.

2 for 1

- Place 1–2 tablespoons of flour in a bowl and mix in the paprika. Dip in the beef chunks and ensure they are thoroughly coated.

- Heat the olive oil in the sauté pan. Add the beef and onion and cook until beef starts to brown.

- Add the red currant jelly and when melted, add the ale. Heat gently before transferring to the slow cooker.

- Add all the remaining stew ingredients (not the dumpling mixture). Place on low heat and cook for 8–10 hours.

- 45 minutes before serving, make the dough into small balls and place these on top of the stew. Cover and leave for 30 minutes, until dumplings fluff up.

- Serve when ready.

Healthy swaps: For gluten-free diets, switch the flours for Doves Farm plain and self raising flours and opt for a gluten-free ale, suet and stock. To reduce the fat content, remove any visible fat from the meat.

● Beef

Serves 4

Beef Bourguignon

Perfect for dinner parties as you can prepare in advance and enjoy being a host while it cooks making it all look effortless.

- Flour the beef before adding to a sauté pan with a little olive oil or coconut oil and cook until browned. Remove from pan and place in your stock pot.

- Add all the remaining ingredients and combine well in the stock pot.

- Place on low and cook for 8–10 hours.

- Serve with mashed potato and steamed green leafy vegetables.

Healthy swap: Speak to your butcher for the best cuts of beef for health as well as slow cook. If you don't want the additional calories for the wine, you could opt for a low cal red wine.

Ingredients:
750g beef steak, diced
1–2 tbsp flour
Olive oil or coconut oil
1 small red onion, diced
1–2 cloves of garlic, roughly chopped (optional)
200g shallots
150g pancetta, diced
2 carrots, diced
1 sweet potato, peeled and diced
1 tin chopped tomatoes
300ml of red wine (ideally Burgundy)
1 tsp dried thyme
2 heaped tsp paprika
1 beef stock (I use Knorr Rich Beef Stock Pot Gel)
150g button mushrooms

Allow 15 minutes to preheat your slow cooker.

Serves 4–6

Simple Steak and Ale Pie

Ingredients:

1kg of braising steak (or lean
  steak)
1 tbsp flour
1 tsp paprika
½ tsp chilli powder
1 large red onion, finely
  chopped
2–3 cloves, finely chopped
2 carrots, diced
½ tsp wholegrain mustard
500ml strong ale
2 squares of dark chocolate
  (at least 70% cocoa solids)
1 beef stock cube (I use Knorr
  Rich Beef stock pots)
300g puff pastry
Milk or beaten egg

Allow 15 minutes to preheat
your slow cooker.

This is a delicious but very rich recipe. I normally make this the day before as I think it is better to let it rest for a day so that the flavours combine but if you cook it in one it is still delicious. I do not brown off the meat. I have tried both ways and to be honest not noticed any difference in flavour, so now opt for the easiest route.

- Dice the steak, removing any visible fat if you are opting for a healthier dish.

- Place the flour, paprika and chilli in a bowl. Dip the steak in this before adding to the stock pot.

- Add the chopped vegetables, ale and stock cubes.

- Cook on auto or low for 8–10 hours.

- 30 minutes before cooking add the chocolate to the slow cooker.

- Roll out your puff pastry. Heat your oven to 200°C. Cut the puff pastry into large wedges – big enough to cover a portion of the meat so it looks like a pie topping.

- Brush with milk or beaten egg.

- Place on your greased baking tray and cook until golden and risen – approximately 20–30 minutes.

● **Beef**

- When ready to serve, add a dollop or two of the meat dish and cover with the puff pastry wedge. Serve with shredded steamed cabbage and mashed potato.

Healthy tip: Opt for the leanest beef you can. Avoid the pastry topping or for a less fattening option, use a few sheets of filo pastry, scrunched up, to form the topping. If you want to cut back on salt, opt for low salt stock cubes.

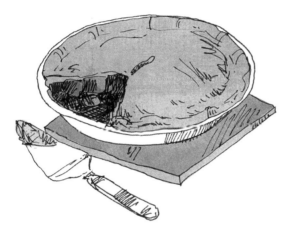

Serves 4

Healthy Beef Curry

Ingredients:

1–3cm knuckle of fresh
  ginger, peeled
3–4 cloves of garlic, chopped
1–3 chillies, depending on
  personal taste and strength
1–2 tbsp olive oil
Small handful coriander leaves
1 tbsp garam masala
½ tsp cumin
2 tsp turmeric
750g beef, diced
½ tsp coconut oil
1 large red onion, chopped (or
  2 medium)
1 pepper, sliced
1 tin chopped tomatoes
200ml water
3 tbsp 0% fat Greek yoghurt
Chopped coriander leaves
Zest of a lime

Allow 15 minutes to preheat
your slow cooker.

You can use this recipe with vegetables, lamb or chicken. This uses beef, which works really well in the slow cooker. Speak to your butcher to find the best beef for the slow cooker and for health.

- In a food processor, add the ginger, garlic, chilli, olive oil, half the coriander leaves, garam masala, cumin and turmeric. Whizz until you form a paste. Leave to one side to rest (store in the fridge or freeze until needed).

- Brown the beef gently in a little coconut oil. Remove and pop into the slow cooker along with all the remaining ingredients apart from the yoghurt, coriander leaves and lime.

- Turn your slow cooker to low and cook for 8–10 hours.

- 20–30 minutes before serving, taste. If you need more spice you can stir in some more garam masala. Add the Greek yoghurt, chopped coriander and the zest of a lime.

- Stir and serve on a bed of rice – ideally brown rice or basmati if you are healthy conscious.

Healthy swap: Want to cut down on your saturated fat from the beef? Swap half the beef for wholesome vegetables and beans.

Beef

Serves 4–6

Beef, Vegetable and Horseradish Casserole

Beef and horseradish work really well together.

- When preparing the vegetables, make sure they are evenly sized as this will ensure an even cook and look better when served.

- Chop the brisket into cubes. Mix the flour and paprika together, season. Dip the beef into the flour ensuring it is evenly coated.

- Heat the coconut oil in your sauté pan. Add the beef and onion and cook until onions starts to soften and the beef browns. Place this into your preheated slow cooker.

- Add all ingredients. Make sure the stock is hot when adding as this will keep the temperature.

- Turn your slow cooker to low and cook for 8–10 hours.

- Serve with mash and green vegetables.

Ingredients:
500g brisket of beef, cubed
25g flour
3 tsp paprika
Coconut or olive oil
1 onion, diced
Half a swede, peeled and cubed
2–3 carrots, sliced
2 potatoes, peeled and diced
1–2 parsnips, peeled and diced
50g pearl barley
2 level tsp horseradish sauce
600ml beef stock

Allow 15 minutes to preheat your slow cooker.

Spaghetti Bolognaise

Ingredients:
Olive or coconut oil
2–3 cloves of garlic, finely
   chopped
1 red onion, finely chopped
1 pepper, finely chopped
75g mushrooms, finely
   chopped
500g lean mince beef
1 tin chopped tomatoes
1–2 tsp tomato puree
150 ml red wine
Mixed herbs to taste

This recipe can be used for spaghetti bolognaise or you could double up the recipe to make other dishes – see Chapter 11, Two for One: Lasagne, page 122; Moussaka, page 124; and Stuffed Tomatoes, page 121.

2 for 1

- Place the coconut oil in the sauté pan. Add the onion and mince. Cook the mince until brown and broken up. Transfer to the slow cooker. Add all remaining ingredients and combine well.

- Place the ingredients in the slow cooker. Set to high and cook for 3–4 hours.

- Remove and serve with spaghetti and top with grated parmesan or refer to Chapter 11, Two for One.

Healthy swap: Opt for lean turkey mince to cut down on your saturated fat.

Serves 4

Reggae Beef

If you like your food with a bit of a kick, you will love this dish. Adjust the spices to suit your palate.

- Place the flour and paprika in a bowl and mix in the beef, coating it well.

- You can brown the beef in a sauté pan if you prefer, in a little coconut or olive oil, but I have found little difference in taste so I tend to take the lazy option.

- Place all the ingredients in the slow cooker combine well and set to low. Cook for 8–10 hours.

- Serve with rice.

Ingredients:

500g beef, cut into thick chunks
1–2 tbsp flour
1 tsp smoked paprika
1 large red onion, diced
2–3 cloves of garlic, roughly chopped
2–3cm knuckle of ginger, finely chopped
1–2 chillies, finely chopped
2 large peppers, sliced
1 carrot, diced
2 sticks of celery, diced
1–2 sweet potatoes, diced
2 tomatoes, diced
1 tbsp curry powder (I use medium)
½ tsp allspice
½ tsp cumin
2 tbsp tomato sauce
1 tin black eyed beans, drained
500ml water or low salt stock

Allow 15 minutes to preheat your slow cooker.

Serves 4–6

Braised Oxtail Casserole

Ingredients:
Olive or coconut oil
1 oxtail, cut into 3–5 cm
   pieces (get your butcher to
   do this)
1 tbsp plain flour
1 large red onion, sliced
3 cloves of garlic, crushed
3 sticks of celery, sliced
2 carrots, diced
1 tin tomatoes, chopped
2 tsp sundried tomato paste
200ml red wine
400ml beef stock, hot
1 bay leaf
½ tsp dried parsley

Allow 15 minutes to preheat
your slow cooker.

Oxtails are cheap to buy and work best when slow cooked, releasing their rich and tasty flavour.

- Run the oxtail pieces under water to moisten them. Mix the flour and paprika together and place in a bowl. Add the oxtail pieces to coat with the flour and paprika mix (depending on how many oxtail pieces you have, you may have to use more flour/paprika).

- Heat the olive or coconut oil in a sauté pan. Add the oxtail pieces and brown for 5 minutes.

- Transfer these to your slow cooker. Add all the remaining ingredients, making sure the stock is hot.

- Place on high and cook for 6–8 hours.

- Serve with green vegetables and mashed potato.

Serves 4

Slow-cooked Beef and Bacon Layer

This is an adaption of an older Mrs Beeton's recipe I discovered. It works perfectly in the slow cooker, though don't use fatty meat or bacon as this can give a unpleasant taste. I brown the beef and then remove any excess fat.

- Prepare the meat and vegetables, making sure they are evenly cut to ensure an even cook.

- Place a little olive oil or coconut oil in the base of your sauté pan. Add the beef and brown gently. Drain off any fat.

- Layer the beef, vegetable slices and bacon in your slow cooker, starting with a layer of vegetables first as these take longest to cook.

- Mix the hot beef stock with the wine, herbs and seasoning. Mix well.

- Pour over the meat and vegetable mix, ensuring it is evenly covered.

- Cook on low for 8–10 hours.

Ingredients:
Olive oil or coconut oil
1 large red onion, sliced
500g brisket of beef, diced
½–1 pack of lean bacon
2 sticks of celery, sliced
1 large carrot, sliced
1 large sweet potato, sliced
2 potatoes, sliced
200ml red wine
500ml beef stock
½ tsp allspice
1 tsp dried thyme
Seasoning

Allow 15 minutes to preheat your slow cooker.

Slow-cooked Beef Roast with Red Wine and Cranberries

Ingredients:
Butter or olive oil
1–2 tbsp flour
1–2 tbsp dried onion
Sea salt and black pepper to season
Beef joint
3 cloves of garlic, crushed
200m red wine
1 tbsp Worcester sauce
2 tbsp soy sauce
3 tbsp maple syrup
150g cranberries

Allow 15 minutes to preheat your slow cooker.

I discovered this simple recipe on a slow cook blog, it is really simple to prepare and creates a very tender joint.

- Rub the joint with a little butter or olive oil. Mix the flour, onion, salt and pepper together. Rub this all over the joint, ensuring that it is thoroughly coated.

- Place the joint in the slow cooker and set to low.

- Mix all remaining ingredients together, apart from the cranberries, and pour the liquid into the slow cooker. Add the cranberries.

- Cover and cook on low for 8–10 hours, until tender.

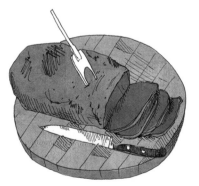

Beef

Serves 4–6

Daube of Beef

Daube of beef is a traditional French stew – normally cooked at various stages over a period of days to make the most of the flavours. You can speed up the marinating process by using a vacuum packer which seals the flavours. This is well worth the preparation for a luxurious stew. Traditionally this would have been made with white wine, but I think red goes much nicer with beef, but the choice is yours.

- Place the wine, brandy, garlic, herbs, orange, onions and sundried tomatoes in your slow cooker pan and combine well. Add the beef and cover. Leave in the fridge overnight to marinate.

- Next morning, remove the beef from the fridge and bring up to room temperature.

- Place the beef and marinade in the slow cooker.

- Add all the remaining ingredients apart from the olives.

- Place on low and cook for 8–10 hours.

- Half an hour before serving, add the olives.

- Remove the cinnamon sticks and orange, season and serve.

Ingredients:
450 ml red wine
2 tbsp brandy
3–4 small red onions, quartered
2 cloves of garlic
2 sticks of cinnamon
2 bay leaves
Sprigs of rosemary and thyme
6–8 sundried tomatoes (in oil, drained)
1 orange, cut into six
2 tsp paprika
500g beef, diced
Olive oil
2 carrots, diced
1 leek, finely diced
1 tin chopped tomatoes
150g button mushrooms, whole
Handful of olives

Allow 15 minutes to preheat your slow cooker.

Guinness and Beef Casserole

Ingredients:

800g lean beef stewing steak

2–3 tbsp flour

2 tsp paprika

Black pepper

2 large red onions, sliced

6–8 shallots, halved

2–3 carrots, diced

1 large parsnip, diced

1 sweet potato, diced

300ml Guinness

1 low salt beef stock cube, dissolved in 100ml hot water

½ tsp dried parsley

½ tsp thyme

1 bay leaf

Allow 15 minutes to preheat your slow cooker.

This is a really filling meal. Serve with mash. You could make this into pies – simply cook as described below. Once cooked, place in individual pie dishes and top with a layer of puff pastry. Bake in the oven until golden (approximately 25–30 minutes at 200°C).

- Dice the beef, removing any fat. Place the flour, paprika and black pepper in a dish. Roll the beef in the flour mixture.

- You can place all the ingredients in the slow cooker, but if you prefer, you can brown the beef first. Place olive oil or coconut oil in a sauté pan. Add the beef and brown. Transfer this to the slow cooker.

- Add all the remaining ingredients. Cover and cook on low for 8 hours.

- Serve with mash and steamed green vegetables.

Serves 4

Beef Goulash

A Goulash is a Hungarian stew, seasoned with paprika – normally smoked. This is my own version of this traditional dish.

- Using your slow cooker pan or a sauté pan, heat the oil and cook the onion, garlic and beef until browned and the onions start to soften. You can ignore this part if you don't want to brown the meat.

- Return this to the slow cooker and add all remaining ingredients apart from the creme fraiche and parsley. Place on high for 3–4 hours, or low for 6 hours.

- Prior to serving add the remaining chopped parsley and stir in the creme fraiche (you can use natural yoghurt, I find that Total Greek Yoghurt is the best).

Ingredients:
Olive or coconut oil
1 red onion, finely sliced
1–2 cloves of garlic, crushed
2 red peppers, finely sliced
500g beef stewing steak, cut into chunks
4 tsp paprika
1 tin chopped tomatoes
1–2 tsp tomato puree
200 ml red wine
200 ml beef stock
Handful of freshly chopped parsley
150 ml creme fraiche

Allow 15 minutes to preheat your slow cooker.

Chilli Con Carne

Ingredients:
400g lean beef mince (or
  pre-drained of fat)
1 onion, finely chopped
Coconut or olive oil
1–2 cloves garlic, crushed
1 red pepper, chopped
1 tin chopped tomato
1 tin red kidney beans
200 ml beef stock
1 tsp chilli powder
1 tsp paprika
1–2 chopped chillies
  (depending on desired
  flavour)
100g mushrooms, quartered
Dash of Worcester sauce
1 tsp ground cumin
Seasoning to taste

A family favourite, you can serve on a bed of rice or use in wraps, tortilla dishes or even as a topping for jacket potatoes. You can double up the recipe and freeze until needed. This recipe can be doubled up to make Spicy Enchilada – see Chapter 11, Two for One, or Chilli Stuffed Peppers on page 129.

2 for 1

- Place onion, pepper, mushrooms and garlic in large sauté pan and cook for 1–2 minutes in a little coconut or olive oil. Add chopped chillies and cook for one more minute. Add mince and cook until brown. The mixture should be cooking in its own liquid, but if a little dry add a small amount of the beef stock.

- Add beef stock, tomatoes, red kidney beans and remaining herbs and spices. Cook for 5 minutes before transferring to the slow cooker.

- Cook on low for 5–6 hours.

- Serve with rice and sour cream.

Top tip: Add 2 squares of dark chocolate to add flavour.

● Beef

Fish

Fish is normally cooked fast so some may question why we would want to use a slow cooker. You may be surprised at what you can do with it and how the fish can taste when cooked this way. It also traps the odours so your kitchen doesn't smell too fishy. Below are some tips when cooking fish – you may want to adapt your own recipes to suit or try something new using this advice. Speak to your fishmonger to discuss the right type of fish for the slow cooker.

General cooking

Cooking fish in the slow cooker can really enhance the flavour. However, you will have to consider cooking times. We are so used to slow cookers fitting around our busy lives, fish recipes might not be so accommodating. Fish does not need long cooking times so you will be looking at a maximum of 3–4 hours and it needs to be eaten straight away as it will dry out if left on warm. This may make it less appealing if you want to prepare your slow cooker to cook all day when you are at work.

Poaching

Poaching fish only takes about 45 minutes on high. Add your fish with the stock or water and simply poach with a few herbs to add flavour.

Shellfish

If you like shellfish, such as prawns, etc., add them towards the end of the cooking time otherwise they may spoil. If cooking on high, this can be in the last 20 minutes. If you are using frozen, make sure they are defrosted completely before adding to the stock pot.

Note: For all of the recipes in this chapter, **if your slow cooker needs to be preheated, turn it on 15 minutes before using**. Refer to your manufacturer's instructions for more information on your specific model temperatures.

CHAPTER 8

Cod and Vegetable Bake

Ingredients:
1 red pepper, seeded and
    chopped
4 shallots, finely chopped
2 courgettes, diced
2–3 large tomatoes, finely
    chopped
fresh tarragon finely chopped
4 large boneless cod fillets
300ml fish stock
Seasoning

The vegetables add great flavour to the cod. Serve with new potatoes and a green salad.

- Prepare the vegetables, and place the vegetables, seasoning and herbs in the base of the slow cooker.

- Place the fish fillets on the top.

- Pour over the stock.

- Cook on high for 2–3 hours.

- Serve with new potatoes and salad.

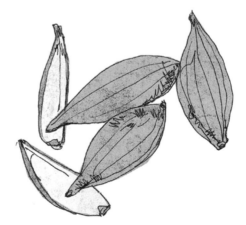

Serves 4

Halibut, Chilli and Vegetable Casserole

Serve this casserole with rice, couscous or quinoa.

- Prepare the vegetables, making sure they are cut to equal size and thickness – ideally chunky.

- Add everything apart from the courgettes and fish to the stock pot. Make sure the fish stock is hot when adding to the stock pot.

- Cook for 6–8 hours on low. Around 45 minutes to 1 hour before serving, switch to high and add the courgette and halibut. Test the fish is tender and cooked before serving.

- Serve with rice, couscous or quinoa.

Ingredients:
1 red onion, sliced
1–2 peppers, sliced
1–2 chillies, finely sliced (to taste)
2 sweet potatoes, peeled and diced
2 small potatoes, peeled and diced
1–2 carrots, diced
2 sticks of celery, diced
1 tin chopped tomatoes
2 tsp sundried tomato paste
½ tsp chilli powder
1 tsp paprika
200ml white wine
200ml fish stock
2 courgettes, thickly sliced
500g halibut fillets, diced

Italian Baked Cod

Ingredients:
12–15 cherry or vine tomatoes
1 large red onion, sliced
Handful of olives, halved or whole
2–3 cloves of garlic
Olive oil
Balsamic vinegar
Sprinkle of sugar
Sprinkle of sea salt (very small!)
2–3 sprigs of thyme
4 cod fillets
Sundried tomato pesto

If you are concerned about using cod, you can opt for a more sustainable fish such as coley or pollock.

- Place the half the tomatoes, onion, olives and garlic in the base of the slow cooker. Drizzle with olive oil, balsamic vinegar followed by a sprinkle of sugar and tiny bit of salt.

- Spread the top of the fillets with a thin layer of pesto. Place these onto of the vegetables.

- Cover with the remaining vegetables and drizzle with a little more oil and balsamic.

- Place on low for 1½–2 hours or until the fish is cooked to taste.

- Serve with a healthy salad and new minted potatoes.

Serves 4

Seafood Aljotta

This is a Maltese fish soup, but as the fish pieces are quite large in this, I think it makes a really nice meal, especially when served with crusty bread, or even new potatoes and green vegetables. This recipe uses fish pieces. You can buy fish pie pieces, which is ideal for this. The normally contain a selection of salmon, haddock, pollack or cod.

- Place all the ingredients in the stock pot apart from the fish pieces and the parsley.

- Cook on high for 1 hour. Add the fish pieces and parsley and cook on high for ½–1 hour, until the fish is cooked to your taste.

- Serve immediately.

Ingredients:
1 onion, finely chopped
1–2 tbsp sundried tomato
    paste
1 tsp paprika
1 bay leaf
1 tin chopped tomatoes
250ml white wine
250ml fish stock
100g rice
350g fish pieces
Handful of fresh parsley,
    finely chopped

Thai Salmon Curry

Ingredients:
1 onion, finely chopped
1-2 cloves of garlic, roughly
    chopped
2cm knuckle of ginger, finely
    chopped
Juice and zest of half a lime
1 tsp Thai fish sauce
2 tbsp Thai curry paste
300ml coconut milk
500g salmon pieces
200g green beans, cut into
    3-4cm lengths

This recipe uses coconut milk which can be quite calorific, so opt for a low fat version if you are watching your weight.

- Place everything apart from the salmon and green beans into the slow cooker.

- Turn to high and cook for 1 hour.

- Add the salmon and green beans and cook for another 45 minutes to 1 hour, until the salmon is cooked to your taste.

- Serve with rice.

Serves 4

Red Snapper and Tomato Bake

Red snapper is packed with protein, selenium, vitamin D and phosphorus.

- In a sauté pan, add the olive or coconut oil and red onion. Fry until starting to become translucent.

- Add the garlic and tomatoes, wine and half the basil to the sauté pan. Cook for another 2–3 minutes.

- Place half the tomato mixture on the base of the slow cooker. Add the fish.

- Pour the remaining tomato mixture over the fish.

- Bake on the low heat for 1–2 hours or until fish is cooked to your taste.

Ingredients:
500g red snapper fillets
Olive or coconut oil
2 cloves of garlic, crushed
1 red onion, finely chopped
50g sundried tomatoes, chopped
3 ripe vine tomatoes, chopped
200ml red wine
Handful of chopped fresh basil

Simple Fish Pot

Ingredients:
2 onions, diced
2–3 cloves of garlic, roughly
   chopped
4 tomatoes, diced
½ tsp ground cumin
1 tsp paprika
2 bay leaves
1 tsp dried parsley
600g mixed fish
500–600ml stock

Fill your stock pot and wait 1–2 hours for a tasty fish pot. You can buy fish pie pieces, which is ideal for this. This dish normally contains a selection of salmon, haddock, pollack or cod.

- Add all the ingredients into the stock pot.

- Place on low and cook for 1 ½–2 hours, or until the fish is done (depending on the size and what type of fish you are using).

- Serve with freshly chopped parsley garnish.

- Fish

Serves 1–2

Slow-cooked Trout

This is a really simple dish, no herbs or thrills, just plain trout cooked in your slow cooker. This is also nice with a few slices of lemon in the base – this gives a subtle lemon flavour to the fish. Timings depend on the size of the trout. Cooking time is 45 minutes to 1½ hours.

Ingredients:
1–2 trouts, gutted, heads and
   tails removed
500ml water

- Place a trivet, wire rack or upturned saucer in the base of the slow cooker.

- Add 500ml warm water.

- Add the trout.

- Cook on high for 45 minutes to 1 ½ hours, depending on size of trout.

- Serve with a green salad and vinaigrette dressing.

Cod with Pea Puree

Ingredients:
300g peas
200ml vegetable stock
2 pieces of cod
1 tbsp low fat creme fraiche
Handful of fresh mint leaves

A light meal, serve with new potatoes and salad. You can replace the cod with any other white fish.

- Place the peas and vegetable stock in the base of the slow cooker.

- Place the cod on the top.

- Cook for 1 ½–2 hours – until the fish is cooked and flakes easily.

- Remove the fish and place on a plate with foil covering it to keep it warm.

- Remove the peas with a slatted spoon – you don't need the stock.

- Puree the peas with the creme fraiche and mint leaves. Use a processor for this. Season to taste.

- Pour the puree over the cod when ready to serve.

Vegetarian

It is really important to have one or two vegetarian meals a week at least. Not only do they help provide you with some of your five a day, but they are packed with fibre and nutrients and are typically lower in fat than meat meals. Fill your store-cupboard with pulses and beans to add nutrients and extra fibre to your meals.

Note: For all of the recipes in this chapter, **if your slow cooker needs to be preheated, turn it on 15 minutes before using**. Refer to your manufacturer's instructions for more information on your specific model temperatures.

Serves 4–6

Goats Cheese, Spinach and Sundried Tomato Frittata

Ingredients:
Olive oil spray
1 red onion, finely chopped
Half jar of sundried tomatoes (in oil, oil drained)
80g spinach leaves
110g goats cheese, crumbled
6 eggs
250ml Greek yoghurt
Few sprigs of fresh oregano, finely chopped
Pepper to taste

My favourite combination – I love goats cheese. Serve hot or cold with a lovely salad.

- Spray the base of the slow cooker well with olive oil. If you are nervous about it sticking you could line with baking parchment, stuck down with the olive oil spray.

- Prepare the vegetables and cheese. Layer these in the slow cooker, ensuring they are evenly combined.

- Beat the eggs and yoghurt together and season with oregano and pepper. Pour this over the vegetables – it will soak through ensuring the whole thing is covered.

- Place on high and cook for 1–2 hours.

- When cooked, remove the pot from the cooker base. Run a sharp knife around the edge to help loosen the frittata. Carefully place a plate on the base of the pot, top of plate facing into the pot and turn so the frittata drops onto the plate.

- Serve hot or cold with salad.

Healthy tip: Frittatas can contain cream but this recipe uses fat-free Greek yoghurt. It is healthier than cooking on the hob as it is not fried.

● Vegetarian

Serves 4–6

Vegetable and Bean Chilli

You don't have to be vegetarian to enjoy this meal. Packed full of nutrients, this is a really wholesome and delicious Chilli. Serve with rice or add it to a jacket potato, pop it in a wrap or simply enjoy on its own with some crusty bread.

- Place all the ingredients into the slow cooker and combine well.

- Cook on low for 8–10 hours.

- Serve with rice and sour cream.

Healthy tip: Chillies contain a chemical called Caspian, which raise the body temperature. A recent study found that eating around 1g a day can help you burn off more calories. Those eating chillies were also found to consume less food as they felt less hungry and had fewer cravings for fatty, salty or sugary foods.

Ingredients:
1 onion, finely chopped
1–2 cloves garlic, crushed
1 red pepper, chopped
2 sticks of celery, diced
2 carrots, diced
1–2 sweet potatoes, diced
1 tin chopped tomatoes
1 tin red kidney beans, drained
1 tin mixed beans, drained
50g red lentils
200ml passata
200ml water
1–2 tsp chilli powder
1 tsp paprika
1–2 chopped chillies (depending on desired flavour)
Seasoning to taste

Serves 2–4

Squash, Sundried Tomato and Goats Cheese Risotto

Ingredients:
Coconut or olive oil
Knob of butter
1 onion, finely chopped
Half squash, cubed
300g risotto rice
500–700ml vegetable stock
200ml white wine
50g sundried tomatoes
120g goats cheese, crumbled
Handful of fresh, chopped
    herbs

Risottos work well in the slow cooker – I love the combination of squash and goats cheese.

- Place a splash of olive oil and a knob of butter in the bottom of a large saucepan or sauté pan. Add the chopped onion and fry until translucent. Add the cubed squash and stir well.

- Add the rice and stir in, ensuring that the rice is completely covered in the oil/butter mixture. Don't let this stick! If necessary keep the heat to a medium rather than full.

- Add the wine and stir thoroughly. The wine will evaporate but will flavour the rice.

- Place the rice mixture into the slow cooker. Add the warm stock

- Cook for 1–2 hours on high. The rice should be tender but not soggy. 15 minutes before serving, stir in the fresh herbs and chopped sundried tomatoes.

- Serve with crumbled goats cheese.

- Vegetarian

Serves 4

Tomato and Vegetable Pilaf

You can eat this on its own or as a side dish. This makes a lovely supper when you are hungry but don't want anything too heavy.

- Cut the vegetables into equal size so you get a more even cook.

- Add all ingredients. Make sure the stock is hot when adding as this will keep the temperature.

- Turn your slow cooker to high and cook for 3 hours.

Healthy tip: Did you know that basmati rice is low GI. Great if you want a healthy option, but don't fancy brown rice. Mix with wild and red rice for contrast and texture.

Ingredients:
1 onion, diced
2 cloves of garlic, roughly
  chopped
1 red pepper, sliced
1 yellow pepper, sliced
1 tin chopped tomatoes, diced
8–10 sundried tomatoes
  (drained from the oil), left
  whole or halved
50g red lentils
250g basmati rice
75g wild and red rice mix
½ tsp chilli powder
Pinch of cayenne pepper
750ml low salt vegetable
  stock

Serves 4–6

Vegetable Cobbler

Ingredients:

Spray of olive oil, or ¼ tsp
   coconut oil
1 tsp coriander seeds
1 onion, diced
1–2 cloves of garlic, roughly
   chopped
2 carrots, diced
1 yellow pepper, diced
2 sweet potatoes, diced
Half butternut squash (or
   small squash), diced
1 tin tomatoes
1 tsp tomato or sundried
   tomato puree
1 can of haricot or chickpeas,
   drained
1 tsp paprika
½ tsp chilli powder

Topping
250g self-raising flour
½ tsp dried parsley or mixed
   herbs
50g butter
100ml buttermilk
1 egg

It is important to have at least two meals a week without meat. This is a great dish for vegetarians as well as meat eaters as it is filling and packed with nutrients.

- Spray a sauté pan with olive oil or add a ¼ tsp of coconut oil. Place the coriander seeds and onion in the sauté pan and cook until the onion starts to soften and the coriander seeds start to become fragrant.

- Cut the vegetables into equal size so you get a more even cook.

- Add all ingredients apart from the topping. Make sure the stock is hot when adding as this will keep the temperature.

- Turn your slow cooker to auto and cook for 6–8 hours, on low for 6–8 hours or if you want a faster meal, turn to high for 4–5 hours.

- 45 minutes before you are ready to serve, you can make the scone/cobbler topping.

- Sift the flour into a bowl and add the herbs. Add the butter and rub to form bread crumbs.

- Mix the buttermilk with the egg and add this to the flour mixture. Add the buttermilk and combine to form a dough firm but not wet, dough.

- Place this on a floured board, and press out until 3–4cm thick. Cut with a pastry cutter. You may have some left over

- Vegetarian

– it depends on how many you place in the slow cooker (see penultimate point below before your proceed).

- Place on top of the casserole. Pop the lid back on and cook for another 30–40 minutes, until risen.

- If you want to darken them, you will need to place under the grill. Alternatively you could cook the scones in the oven separately and add them when plating up.

- Serve with a garnish of fresh parsley.

Healthy swap: You can turn this into a vegetable stew if you don't fancy the cobber/scone topping. For those following a wheat or gluten free diet, swap the flour for Doves Farm Gluten Free.

Serves 4

Lentil Dahl

Ingredients:
1 onion, chopped
2 cloves garlic, crushed
1 pepper, chopped (optional)
100g red lentils
1–2 inch knuckle of fresh
　ginger
3 heaped tsp mild or sweet
　curry powder
1–2 tsp turmeric
3 tomatoes, finely chopped
1 tsp tomato puree
300–400ml of hot water
2 tbsp low fat creme fraiche
　or 0% fat Greek yoghurt
　(optional)

This is so easy to make and costs very little. You can make it mild and creamy by adding some Greek yoghurt – ideal for children or spice it up to suit your taste. You can add fresh chillies or chilli flakes if you prefer a more powerful dahl.

- Add all ingredients apart from the creme fraiche/yoghurt.

- Turn your slow cooker to auto and cook for 6–8 hours, on low for 6–8 hours or if you want a faster meal, turn to high for 4–5 hours.

- Stir occasionally during cooking. You may need to add more liquid if it needs it.

- If you like a creamier dahl, stir in a couple of tablespoons of creme fraiche or Greek yoghurt. Sprinkle with coconut before serving.

Healthy tip: Lentils can help lower cholesterol and help balance blood sugars. They are an excellent source of protein, fibre, B vitamins and minerals.

Vegetarian

Serves 4–6

Moroccan Style Vegetable Tagine with Quinoa

A really wholesome dish with a kick. Serve with quinoa as this is much better nutritionally than the traditional couscous.

- Add all ingredients. Make sure the stock is hot when adding as this will keep the temperature.

- Turn the slow cooker to low and cook gently for 8–10 hours.

- Serve with quinoa and a garnish of freshly chopped coriander and flaked almonds.

Healthy tip: Quinoa is a complete protein that will keep you fuller for longer, helping you with weight loss, but it has also been shown to protect you against some cancers. It contains more iron than other grains and a very good source of fibre. A study found a diet rich in grains such as Quinoa offers significant protection against cancer, in pre-menopausal women. High in protein and contains good quantities of phosphorus and potassium. It is also a really rich source of vitamin E.

Ingredients:
1 red onion, diced
2–3 cloves of garlic, roughly chopped
1 chilli, finely chopped
2cm knuckle of ginger, finely chopped
2 peppers, diced
2 carrots, diced
2 sweet potatoes, peeled and diced
1 white potato, peeled and diced
1 tin chopped tomatoes
1 tin chickpeas, drained
40g dried apricots, halved
1–2 tsp chilli powder
½ tsp chilli flakes (optional)
2 tsp turmeric
½ tsp ground cinnamon
½ tsp dried mint
½ tsp ground coriander
200ml hot water

Mushroom Risotto

Ingredients:
Coconut or olive oil
Knob of butter
1 onion, finely chopped
10g dried porcini mushrooms
400g mixed mushrooms
(shiitake, oyster, chestnut, wild, etc.)
300g risotto rice
500ml stock/mushroom water
200ml white wine
Zest of half a lemon
Handful of fresh tarragon, chopped
2-3 spoonfuls of low fat creme fraiche or 0% fat Greek yoghurt
Handful of fresh, chopped herbs

Perfect for a tasty lunch or even a starter.

- Soak porcini mushrooms as directed on pack. This normally takes 20 minutes. Retain the fluid to add to your stock.

- Place a splash of olive oil and a knob of butter in the bottom of a large saucepan or sauté pan. Add the chopped onion and fry until translucent. Add the fresh and dried mushrooms, stir well.

- Add the rice and stir in, ensuring that the rice is completely covered in the oil/butter mixture. Don't let this stick. If necessary keep the heat to a medium rather than full.

- Add the wine and stir thoroughly. The wine will evaporate but will flavour the rice.

- Place everything into the slow cooker. Add the warm stock.

- Cook for 1–2 hours on high. The rice should be tender but not soggy. When ready to serve, stir in the tarragon and lemon zest. For creamy risotto, stir in the creme fraiche or Greek yoghurt.

- Serve immediately, garnished with chopped herbs and parmesan.

Vegetarian

Serves 4

Tuscan Tomato and Beans

One of my favourite lunches. Packed with protein and fibre – a great slow release energy meal.

- Add all the ingredients apart from the feta cheese and combine well. Add more stock if needed.

- Set the temperature to low and cook for 8–10 hours.

- Serve with a sprinkle of fresh parsley, crumbled feta cheese and warm crusty bread.

Ingredients:
1kg tomatoes, chopped
1 large red onion, chopped
2-3 cloves of garlic, roughly
    chopped
1 red pepper, diced
1 stick of celery, diced
200ml red wine or stock
2 tins borlotti or cannellini
    beans, drained (or one of
    each)
½ tsp dried thyme
½ tsp dried oregano
1 tsp dried parsley
1 tsp sugar
Sprinkle of salt and pepper
1 tsp balsamic vinegar
    (optional)
Fresh parsley, chopped (for
    garnish)
100g feta cheese, crumbled

Serves 2–4

Beetroot Risotto

Ingredients:
Coconut or olive oil
Knob of butter
1 red onion, finely chopped
2 cloves of garlic, crushed
200g cooked beetroot, cut
   into chunks
300g risotto rice
500ml low salt vegetable
   stock
200ml red wine
20g parmesan cheese, grated

This is an amazing vibrant red risotto that looks really dramatic. Top with dark green lettuce leaves such as rocket to help emphasis the fabulous colour.

- Place a splash of olive oil and a knob of butter in the bottom of a large saucepan or sauté pan. Add the chopped onion and garlic and fry until translucent. Add the beetroot chunks and stir well. Cook for 5–8 minutes to help the beetroot soften.

- Add the rice and stir in, ensuring that the rice is completely covered in the oil/butter mixture. Don't let this stick. If necessary keep the heat to a medium rather than full.

- Add the wine and stir thoroughly. The wine will evaporate but will flavour the rice.

- Place the rice mixture into the slow cooker. Add the warm stock.

- Cook for 1–2 hours on high. The rice should be tender but not soggy. When ready to serve, stir in the parmesan. Serve immediately.

Healthy tip: Beetroot is high in fibre, potassium, vitamins A, C and B6 as well as being a good source of magnesium and iron. Known as a blood purifier, it has also been shown to help reduce heart disease, strokes and high blood pressure.

Vegetarian

Cashew and Mushroom Stuffed Peppers

A delicious combination, easy to prepare.

Ingredients:
Coconut or olive oil
120g mushrooms (chestnut or a mixture)
1 red onion
80g cashew nuts
2 slices of wholemeal bread (or gluten-free bread)
1-2 tsp yeast extract (Marmite or similar)
½ tsp dried parsley
4 peppers
500ml hot vegetable stock

- In a food processor, add the mushrooms and whizz until they are finely chopped. Do the same for the onion, nuts and bread.

- Place a little coconut or olive oil in a pan. Add the mushrooms and onions and cook until they start to soften. Add the remaining ingredients apart from the peppers and stock and cook for 5–10 minutes.

- Cut the tops off the peppers and leave to one side (you will add these again when stuffed). Carefully remove the seeds from the peppers.

- Place the mushroom mixture in each pepper. Top with the pepper tops.

- Place them in the base of the slow cooker. Carefully pour the hot stock into the base of the slow cooker (around the peppers not over them).

- Leave to cook on high for 1 ½–2 hours or low for 4 hours.

- Remove the peppers from the stock and serve with a delicious salad.

Vegetable Korma

Ingredients:
2 tbsp olive oil
2 cloves of garlic
2–3cm knuckle of ginger
2–3 tomatoes
1 tbsp ground almonds
1–2 tbsp korma curry powder
1 tbsp garam masala
½ tsp cumin
½ tsp turmeric
¼ tsp nutmeg
1 large onion, diced
1 pepper, diced
2 sweet potatoes, peeled and diced
2 potatoes, peeled and diced
1 large carrot, diced
½ head of cauliflower
1 tin chickpeas, drained
300–450ml vegetable stock or water
2–3 handfuls of baby leaf spinach
2 courgettes, thickly sliced
4–5 tbsp thick 0% fat Greek yoghurt

Forget the calorie laden kormas – this is a great recipe for vegetarians and meat eaters. I like to make a selection of curries and serve together so you can mix up the flavours. If you love curries, double up the recipes in this book and freeze smaller portions ready to make a lovely selection and invite friends for a curry night. They will be impressed by all your hard work and all you have to do is reheat and enjoy the atmosphere.

- In your food processor, add the oil, garlic, ginger, spices and tomatoes and whizz until you form a paste.

- Chop the vegetables so they are roughly all the same size.

- Place the vegetables (but not the spinach or courgettes) and chickpeas in the slow cooker. Pour on the paste and 300ml stock/water and combine well. Add more stock if you need to but remember the stock does not evaporate so if you want a thicker sauce, don't add too much (if during cooking you think you have added too much water, mix some cornflour with water to form a paste and mix into the korma – alternatively throw in a large handful of red lentils).

- Place on low and cook for 6–8 hours. 1 hour before serving, mix in the spinach, courgettes and Greek yoghurt. Turn to high and continue to cook for the remaining hour.

- Serve with rice and Indian chutneys.

Serves 4

Vegetable and Chickpea Crumbly

This is a very filling meal – you really don't need to serve it with anything else. Prepare the base in the slow cooker, then add the crumbly topping and pop under the grill. I love the crunchy topping. We normally fight over this in our house.

- Place all the ingredients, apart from the crumbling topping ingredients, in the slow cooker. Place on low and cook for 8 hours.

- When ready to serve, mix the crumbly topping together. Remove the stock pot from the slow cooker. Place the crumbly topping over the vegetable mix and place this under the grill until golden.

- Serve immediately.

Ingredients:
Olive oil
2 red onions, cut into wedges
2 cloves of garlic, crushed
1 leek, sliced
1 large carrot, diced
2 sticks of celery, diced
2 sweet potatoes, thickly diced
1 white potato, thickly diced
1 tin chopped tomatoes
2 tsp sundried tomato paste
2 tsp paprika
Handful of freshly chopped parsley
300ml vegetable stock
1 tin chickpeas, drained

Crumbly Topping
100g oats
250g breadcrumbs
50g seed mix
75g parmesan or mature cheddar, grated

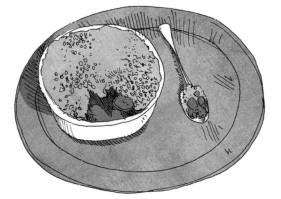

CHAPTER 10

Cheats' Dishes

Sometimes all you want to do is take the simple option. The supermarkets are packed with helpful jars and packs to help you on your way. We are not talking junk food here – just a helping hand occasionally. You can still make healthy choices and add fresh ingredients to a dish without breaking too much of a sweat. These recipes use fresh ingredients with an added cheat to make your life easier but still deliver the taste you want. Always read the labels and check the fat, sugar and salt content. You will be surprised, sometimes the own brands are actually healthier than leading brands – as well as being kinder to your pocket!

Note: For all of the recipes in this chapter, **if your slow cooker needs to be preheated, turn it on 15 minutes before using.** Refer to your manufacturer's instructions for more information on your specific model temperatures.

Serves 4–6

Cheat's Quick Chilli

If you like chilli but a bit scared about adding all the spices to create the best flavour, you can cheat with a chilli paste. You can of course buy powder chilli mixes, but I prefer the pastes as they create a more homemade feel.

Ingredients:
500g lean mince beef
1 large onion, finely chopped
1 large pepper, chopped
1 tin red kidney beans, drained
1 tin chopped tomatoes
1 jar of chilli con carne paste (I like Very Lazy Chilli Con Carne Concentrate)

- You can brown the beef if you prefer, this is ideal if you want to drain off any excess fat, avoiding a fatty flavour to the dish.

- Add all the ingredients and combine well. You should not need any liquid but if you feel it needs something, add a small amount of water. Remember the slow cooker does not evaporate liquid.

- Cook for 5–6 hours on low or 2–3 on high.

- Serve with rice and sour cream.

Serves 4–6

Cheat's Chicken and Vegetable Curry

Ingredients:
3-4 chicken breasts
1 large red onion, finely
    chopped
1 pepper, diced
2 sweet potatoes, diced
1 white potato, diced
50g red lentils
1 tin chickpeas, drained
1 large jar of curry sauce (I
    use Balti)
150g spinach

Allow 15 minutes to preheat
your slow cooker.

This a really easy dish – no messing about with herbs and spices as you can use a jar. Simply chop and go. The beans, lentils and vegetables add to the nutritional value, making this a healthy dish.

- Remove any visible fat from the chicken. Dice evenly.

- Prepare the vegetables and dice evenly.

- Place the chicken and vegetables in the slow cooker. Add the lentils and chickpeas.

- Pour in the curry sauce (see next bullet point below before you do this). Refill the jar half full of water and shake, before pouring into the slow cooker.

- Place on auto as this brings up the temperature quickly, before it automatically switches to low for the remainder of the cooking time. If you don't have an automatic setting, heat up the curry sauce with the water as this will speed up the heating time.

- Cook on auto or low for 8–10 hours.

- 20 minutes before serving, add the spinach. This will give you enough time to cook the rice.

- Serve with brown or basmati rice, mango chutney and naan bread.

● **Cheats' Dishes**

Healthy swap: Opt for the best curry sauce you can find – check the label to see the fat and salt content. If you would like to make your own curry paste, refer to the recipe Simple Chicken Curry in Chapter 4, Poultry, and make your own curry paste – if you do this, add 500ml of boiling water to the paste. Serve with brown rice or basmati.

Serves 4

Cheat's Chicken Tikka

Ingredients:
400g Greek yoghurt
1 tsp turmeric
1 onion, very finely chopped
2 cloves garlic, finely chopped
½ lime, zest and juice
1 chilli, finely chopped
   (optional)
3-4 tbsp tikka paste
4 chicken breasts, diced

Allow 15 minutes to preheat
your slow cooker.

This is a really simple way to cook chicken tikka. I use Greek yoghurt as it holds better than natural yoghurt. Serve on a bed of rice with some extra sauce for dressing.

- In a bowl, combine the yoghurt, turmeric, onion, garlic, lime zest and juice and tikka paste. Add the chilli if you like it hot. Combine well before adding the chicken breasts to the bowl. Cover well with the tikka sauce. Cover the bowl with clingfilm and place in the fridge to marinate overnight or for at least one hour.

- When ready to cook, remove the chicken from the fridge and allow it to come to room temperature.

- 15 minutes before cooking, preheat your slow cooker. Refer to your manufacturer's instructions.

- Add all the ingredients to the slow cooker and cook on high for 3–4 hours.

- Serve on a bed of rice. Reheat any leftover sauce and pour this over the chicken prior to serving.

Cheats' Dishes

Serves 4

Reggae Reggae Chicken

A really simple dish – perfect when you want a lazy meal packed with flavour.

- Place the coconut or olive oil in a sauté pan. Add the chicken and cook for 5 minutes.

- Place the chicken, onion, peppers, sauce and water in the slow cooker.

- Turn to high and cook for 4–5 hours.

- Serve with rice.

Ingredients:
Coconut or olive oil
500g chicken fillets, diced
1 onion, finely chopped
2 peppers, sliced or diced
1 jar of reggae reggae cooking sauce
150ml water

Allow 15 minutes to preheat your slow cooker.

Serves 4

Tomato and Pepper Gnocchi

Ingredients:

1 onion, diced

2–3 cloves of garlic, roughly chopped

2 peppers, sliced

2 tins chopped tomatoes,

1 tbsp sundried tomato paste

½ tsp dried oregano

½ tsp dried parsley

400g fresh gnocchi

110g crumbled feta

2–3 generous handfuls of baby leaf spinach

A great dish if you want some time to entertain your friends. Once the base is made in the slow cooker, it takes less than 10 minutes to finish. You can buy readymade gnocchi from the chilled aisle in the supermarket. Prepare the base sauce in the slow cooker, which can be made in 1–2 hours or on low if you want more time, for 3–4 hours.

- Place all the ingredients apart from the gnocchi, feta and spinach, in the slow cooker. Season to taste.

- Place on low for 4–6 hours or high for 2–3 hours.

- Ten minutes before you are ready to serve, place the spinach in the slow cooker.

- Place the gnocchi in a pan of boiling water for 3–4 minutes. They will bob to the top of the pan when cooked. Remove with a slated spoon so the water drains off.

- Place the gnocchi straight into the slow cooker, leave for 10 minutes.

- Place in serving bowls and sprinkle with the crumbled feta.

Serves 4

Arrabiata Chicken Pasta

A great meal that kids and teenagers love.

- You can brown the chicken if you prefer in a sauté pan with the chilli oil – if you don't want to do this you can move on to the next step (you don't need the oil).

- Add all the ingredients apart from the pasta into the slow cooker.

- Place on high and cook for 3–4 hours or low for 6 hours.

- 20 minutes before you want to serve, place a pan of boiling water on the hob.

- Cook the pasta as per the manufacturer's instructions.

- Once cooked, drain and stir into the slow cooker.

- Serve immediately.

Healthy swap: You can swap the chicken for turkey fillet pieces for a lower fat version. Switch to wholemeal pasta for a healthier option.

Ingredients:
Chilli oil
3–4 chicken fillets, diced
1 onion, sliced
2 red peppers, sliced
1 red chilli, finely sliced
1 tin chopped tomatoes
2–3 cloves of garlic, roughly chopped
1 jar of pasta sauce (ideally chilli and tomato)
1 tin chopped tomatoes
300g penne pasta

Allow 15 minutes to preheat your slow cooker.

CHAPTER
11

Two for One

Make the most of your slow cooker by planning ahead, making two or three different dishes from one recipe and using your freezer. This will not only save you masses of time but will also save you money. This chapter shows you how to adapt existing recipes to make one, two or even three more dishes. If you have a large slow cooker, this can save you masses of time and energy. Most dishes can be frozen or stored in the fridge until needed. For example, your basic bolognaise can be adapted to make a lasagne, moussaka or even a chilli. Chillies can be served with rice or why not fill taco shells or top a jacket potato? Your favourite steak and ale casserole can be made into delicious steak and ale pies. Rice pudding can become a healthy rice brulee.

Top tips

- Always remember to defrost any food thoroughly before placing in the slow cooker.

- Remember the base of your recipe has been previously cooked, so the other advantage of this is a reduction of cooking time.

- Most recipes listed in this chapter detail using the conventional oven and the slow cooker, so you can choose what suits you best.

- Remember to follow standard health and safety advice when reheating foods – especially meat and fish.

Note: For all of the recipes in this chapter, **if your slow cooker needs to be preheated, turn it on 15 minutes before using.** Refer to your manufacturer's instructions for more information on your specific model temperatures.

Serves 4

Spaghetti Bolognaise/ Stuffed Tomatoes

Double up the recipe for bolognaise. You can freeze this or store. Transform into stuffed tomatoes. Follow the Spaghetti Bolognaise recipe found on page 78. This recipe can be made in the slow cooker or oven baked.

Ingredients:
4 large tomatoes
Bolognaise
300ml vegetable stock hot
(not needed when baking in the oven)
110g goats cheese (or mozzarella), crumbled

Slow cooker

- Heat the bolognaise gently in a pan or microwave (you don't have to do this if you are cooking in the oven).

- Cut the tops off the tomatoes and scoop out the middles – you can stir this in to the bolognaise mix to avoid wastage.

- Fill the tomatoes with the warm bolognaise mixture.

- Place in the slow cooker and gently add the stock around the tomatoes.

- Cook for 1–2 hours on high or 3–4 hours on low.

- Remove the tomatoes. Crumble some cheese onto the top and place under the grill for 5 minutes until golden.

- Serve with a salad.

Oven cook: The recipe above uses the slow cooker, but if you want to cook this in the traditional oven, preheat to 200°C. Stuff the tomatoes as directed. Top with the cheese and bake, without the added stock, in the oven for 20–25 minutes until golden.

Spaghetti Bolognaise/ Lasagne

Ingredients:
Bolognaise (from basic recipe)
25g butter
1 heaped tbsp plain flour or
    corn flour
500ml milk
¼ tsp mustard (optional)
Seasoning to taste
Lasagne sheets (ensure it
    says no pre-cook required
    on pack)
Grated cheese to garnish

Take your basic bolognaise recipe found on page 78. You can cook the lasagne in the slow cooker or your standard oven.

- Place butter in saucepan and melt gently on medium heat (not high). Add flour or corn flour and stir well with a wooden spoon. Add a little milk at a time, continuing to stir to avoid lumps.

- Switch now to a balloon whisk. Continue to stir over medium heat until sauce begins to thicken. The balloon whisk will also help eradicate any lumps that may have materialised. Add more milk as necessary to get desired thickness. It should be the thickness of custard.

- Add mustard and season with black pepper.

- Heat the bolognaise gently in a pan or microwave (you don't have to do this if you are cooking in the oven).

- Spray the slow cooker with olive oil as this helps prevent the lasagne from sticking.

- Place a layer of bolognaise mix in the bottom of the slow cooker, then add a thin layer of sauce, finally adding a layer of lasagne sheets. Continue this again, finishing with the sauce. Grate cheese on the top of the sauce, season and sprinkle with some Italian herbs.

- Place the slow cooker on high for 2–3 hours or low and cook for 4–5 hours (until lasagne sheets are cooked).

- If you like a golden topping, you can place the inner stock pot under the grill for five minutes before serving – you may want to add more cheese first.

- Serve with salad and garlic bread.

Oven cook: The recipe above details how to cook in the slow cooker, however, if you want to bake this in a conventional oven, preheat your oven to 200°C, follow the instructions above, placing in an ovenproof dish rather than the stockpot and cook for 30–40 minutes until golden and bubbling.

Spaghetti Bolognaise/ Moussaka

Ingredients:
Basic bolognaise mix
2–3 aubergines, sliced
2 tsp cinnamon powder
1 tsp dried mint
300ml low fat creme fraiche
50g mature cheddar or
   parmesan cheese
Seasoning

You would normally make this with lamb mince, but really the basic recipe works fine with lamb, beef, turkey or even quorn mince. Use the bolognaise recipe on page 78. This recipe can be cooked in the slow cooker or oven cooked.

- In pan of boiling water, add the sliced aubergines for 2 minutes. Take out and pat dry. Leave to one side.

- Preheat the slow cooker following your manufacturer's instructions.

- Mix the mint and cinnamon into the bolognaise.

- Spray olive oil around the inside of the stock pot to prevent sticking.

- Heat the bolognaise gently in a pan or microwave (you don't have to do this if you are cooking in the oven). Place layer of mince in slow cooker, followed by a layer of aubergine. Finish with layer of mince.

- Place on low and cook for 3–4 hours, or high for 2 hours.

- 1 hour before serving, mix the creme fraiche or yoghurt with the eggs and grated cheese. Season with black pepper and pour over the final layer of mince. Garnish with a sprinkle of parmesan and cook for another hour.

- If you want a golden top, place under a grill for 5–10 minutes before serving.

- Serve with a healthy salad.

Oven cook: The recipe above details how to cook in the slow cooker, however, if you want to bake this in a conventional oven, preheat your oven to 200°C, follow the details above, placing in your ovenproof dish rather than the slow cooker. Cook for 30–40 minutes until golden and bubbling.

Serves 4

Irish Lamb Stew/Lamb Hotpot

Ingredients:
Irish lamb stew recipe
3–4 potatoes, washed, not peeled
Sprinkle of grated cheese
Black pepper

Double up the recipe for a lamb stew. You can freeze this or store. Transform into a lamb hotpot. Follow the Irish Lamb Stew recipe found on page 60.

- You don't want to overcook the lamb stew as it has already been cooked, so it is best to use cooked potatoes for this recipe. I boil the potatoes whole in their skins until they are just starting to soften.

- While the potatoes are cooking, warm the stew gently in a pan or microwave before placing in the base of your slow cooker – you don't have to do this if you are cooking this in your conventional oven.

- Slice the potatoes and place these on top of the stew. Finish with a sprinkle of grated cheese and black pepper.

- You can cook on high for 1–2 hours. If you want the top to be golden and crunchy, remove the base from the slow cooker and place under the grill until golden.

- Serve immediately.

Oven cook: The recipe above uses the slow cooker but if you want to cook this in the traditional oven, preheat to 200°C and cook for 20–30 minutes until golden.

Serves 4

Beef and Ale Stew/Beef and Ale Pies

Double up the recipe for beef and ale stew, without the dumplings!
You can freeze this, store in the fridge or remove to make the beef and ale
pies and freeze these uncooked until needed. Follow the Beef and Ale Stew
recipe found on page 72.

Ingredients:
1 large or 4 individual pie
  dishes, greased
Beef and ale mixture
200g puff pastry
1 egg, beaten

- Preheat your oven to 200°C.

- Roll out your puff pastry to your required thickness (or you
  may prefer to use ready rolled). If you want to adhere the
  edge better, you could place a strip of pastry around the lip
  of the pie dish, 'gluing' it in place with some beaten egg.
  Place the pastry over the whole of the pie dish and contents
  and press firmly around the edge to secure.

- Finish with a brush of beaten egg and sprinkle of black
  pepper. You can freeze these uncooked or continue to the
  next stage to cook them.

- Place in the oven and cook for 30–40 minutes until golden
  and bubbling.

Healthy tip: Use filo pastry instead of puff if you want to cut
down on calorie count.

Chilli Con Carne/Spicy Enchilada

Ingredients:
Chilli con carne
1 jar of passata
1 pack of floured tortillas
250g natural Greek yoghurt or
  soured cream
200g mature cheddar

Double up the recipe for chilli con carne. You can freeze this or store. Transform into a spicy enchilada. Follow the Chilli Con Carne recipe found on page 86.

- Place a half of the jar of passata in the base of the slow cooker.

- Place the floured wraps on a board and add a little of the chilli. Wrap well and place each one in the slow cooker.

- Pour the rest of the passata over the wraps.

- Mix the yoghurt or soured cream with the cheddar – season to taste. Pour this over the wraps.

- Place on high for 1–1 ½ hours.

- Serve immediately.

Oven cook: The recipe above uses the slow cooker but if you want to cook this in the traditional oven, preheat to 200°C, follow the recipe above before placing in an ovenproof dish and cook for 20–30 minutes until golden.

Serves 4

Chilli Con Carne/ Stuffed Peppers

These are really delicious when served with a lovely salad – perfect for alfresco dining!

Ingredients:
Chilli con carne
4 peppers
110g goats cheese or
   mozzarella
300ml vegetable stock (only if
   using a slow cooker)

- Warm up the chilli con carne gently in a pan or microwave.

- Cut the tops off the peppers and leave to one side (you will add these again when stuffed). Carefully remove the seeds from the peppers.

- Place the chilli mixture in each pepper. Top with the pepper tops.

- Place them in the base of the slow cooker. Carefully pour the hot stock into the base of the slow cooker (around the peppers not over them).

- Leave to cook on high for 1 ½ –2 hours on low for 4 hours.

- Remove the peppers from the stock. Remove the tops and add the goats cheese or mozzarella. If you want the cheese golden, place under a grill for 3–5 minutes or use a kitchen blow torch to brown. You can replace the tops of the peppers if you wish. Serve with a delicious salad.

Oven cook: The recipe below uses the slow cooker, but if you want to cook this in the traditional oven, preheat to 190°C. Stuff the peppers as directed below. Top with the cheese and bake, without the added stock, in the oven for 20–25 minutes until golden.

Poached Rhubarb/ Nutty Rhubarb Crumble

Ingredients:
Poached rhubarb
200g plain flour
125g butter or margarine
75g brown sugar
30g oats
50g chopped nuts

Double up the recipe for poached rhubarb. You can freeze this or store. Transform into nutty rhubarb crumble. Follow the Poached Rhubarb recipe found on page 162. This recipe is cooked in a conventional oven.

- Preheat the oven to 180°C.

- Place the rhubarb in the base of a deep ovenproof dish.

- In a bowl, rub the flour with the butter to form a mix that resembles breadcrumbs. Stir in the remaining ingredients.

- Place this over the rhubarb base.

- Pop in the oven and cook for 20–25 minutes.

- Serve with custard, ice-cream or for a healthy option, a dollop of fat-free Greek yoghurt.

Serves 4

Rice Pudding/ Raspberry Rice Brulee

This recipe came about from one of those random accidents that can happen in the kitchen. I had some raspberries and thought it would be tasty with the rice, so popped some in a ramekin and covered it with rice. The topping just adds a nice touch. Follow the Rice Pudding recipe found on page 160.

Ingredients:
Rice pudding
Raspberries (frozen works really well)
Brown sugar

- Heat the rice pudding until hot.

- While that is heating up, place the thawed or fresh raspberries in the base of your ramekin dishes.

- Add the hot rice pudding.

- Cover with a brown sugar before using your kitchen blow torch and heating until caramelised.

- Serve hot or cold.

Serves 6–8

Poached Rhubarb/ Rhubarb and Ginger Upside Down Cake

Ingredients:
Poached rhubarb
150g butter
150g sugar
3 eggs
150g self-raising flour
1 tsp ground ginger
30ml milk

Double up the recipe for poached rhubarb. You can freeze this or store. Transform into rhubarb and ginger upside down cake. Follow the Poached Rhubarb recipe found on page 162. This recipe is cooked in a conventional oven.

- Preheat the oven to 180°C.

- Line the springform tin (I use a 20–23cm tin) with a cake liner or with baking parchment.

- Place the rhubarb in the base of the tin (drain off excess liquid). You don't need much rhubarb. To make this look nicer, try to place the rhubarb sticks in to a uniform pattern.

- In a mixing bowl, add all the ingredients and beat well until combined.

- Pour this onto the rhubarb. Press down and spread to make an even cover.

- Pop in the oven and cook for 20–30 minutes until golden. The sponge should spring back when touched.

- Remove from the oven and leave to cool for 5 minutes.

- Place your serving dish upside down (face down) onto the top of the cake tin. Using oven gloves, hold both the tin and the serving dish and flip over. The cake should drop onto the serving dish. Remove the lining.

- Sprinkle with icing sugar and serve hot or cold.

Serves 6–8

Mulled Poached Pears/ Pear and Chocolate Upside Down Cake

Ingredients:

2-3 poached pears (drained of any liquid)
80g sugar
20g butter
150g butter
150g sugar or xylitol
3 eggs
120g flour
30g cocoa
30ml milk

Double up the recipe for mulled poached pears – if you want the poached pears to be less spicy, you can use grape juice, water or white wine instead of the mulled wine. Add a vanilla pod for extra sweetness. Transform into pear and chocolate upside down cake. Follow the Mulled Poached Pears recipe found on page 166.

- Preheat the oven to 190°C.

- I use a cake liner as this prevents sticking, and I put this in a 20–23cm springform tin.

- Place the 80g of sugar in a saucepan and heat carefully. Do not stir. It will start to caramelise and start to change to a golden colour. Once it has coloured, remove from heat and add the 20g of butter. Be very careful as this is very hot.

- Stir in the remaining butter. Once melted in, pour this into the base of the lined cake tin.

- Slice the pears and place them in a nice pattern in the base of the cake tin.

- In a mixing bowl, add all the remaining ingredients. Beat well until you have formed a cake batter.

- Place this over the pears and smooth out the top.

- Pop in the oven and cook for 20–30 minutes until golden. The sponge should spring back when touched.

- Remove from the oven and leave to cool for 5 minutes.

- Place your serving dish upside down (face down) onto the top of the cake tin. Using oven gloves, hold both the tin and the serving dish and flip over. The cake should drop onto the serving dish. Remove the lining.

- Sprinkle with icing sugar and serve hot or cold.

Healthy tip: Swap sugar for xylitol. If you want a gluten free sponge, swap the flour for Doves Farm Self-Raising.

Serves 4–6

Lemon Pavlova Cups

Ingredients:
Lemon curd
Vanilla ice-cream
Limoncello liqueur (optional)
Meringue nests
Thick double cream (optional)

A really delicious and very grown up dessert. I adore lemon puddings and this really does deliver. Follow the recipe for Lemon Curd in this book, on page 178. I like to use homemade meringues as they are chewier than the more powdery shop bought versions, but really, this is delicious whatever you choose. You will not need the all the quantities in the recipe – the amounts depend on how big your serving dishes or glasses are. Remember this is very rich so don't make them too big!

Healthy swap: Swap the ice-cream for a low fat version. The cream can be substituted with low fat creme fraiche or 0% fat natural Greek yoghurt.

- Place a little lemon curd in the base of each of your serving glasses.

- Follow this with a small layer of the vanilla ice-cream, crumbled meringue and cream. Drizzle with limoncello before repeating again.

- Finish with some ice-cream or cream, followed by a drizzle of the lemon curd.

- Serve immediately.

Desserts

We all love great desserts. The slow cooker can be used to make delicious puddings, desserts and even cakes.

Healthy tip

You don't have to avoid desserts if you are watching you weight, simply make some food swaps to the traditional recipe and you can have a guilt free pudding or cake. I would advise swapping the sugar for xylitol, stevia or a stevia blend. Xylitol and stevia are natural sugar alternatives (not artificial sweeteners). Stevia is very sweet so you may want to reduce what you use but xylitol is pretty much like for like so an easy swap. You can buy a stevia blend which is half sugar half stevia, so a good compromise if you want to cut back on sugar. All are available from supermarkets and health food shops. You may also want to swap white flour for wholemeal (see Chapter 2, Healthy Eating Tips for more information on carbohydrates and sugar alternatives). For baking, I still prefer to use butter or stork as I find very low fat margarines can alter the recipe. To accompany your dessert, opt for natural fat-free Greek yoghurt instead of cream. You can also try low fat creme fraiche. If you want to make it sweeter, simply add some low GI syrup or for a lovely vanilla sweet flavour, some vanilla extract or paste.

Note: For all of the recipes in this chapter, **if your slow cooker needs to be preheated, turn it on 15 minutes before using.** Refer to your manufacturer's instructions for more information on your specific model temperatures.

CHAPTER 12

Serves 4

Steamed Raisin and Apple Pudding

Ingredients:
75g butter/low fat margarine
75g brown sugar/xylitol
Zest of one lemon
2 eggs
150g self-raising flour
100g raisins
2 cooking apples, peeled and
  diced
2 tsp ground cinnamon
Generous grating of nutmeg
Grease 1.2 litre pudding basin

Sponge puddings are one of the ultimate comfort foods. Apple, raisin and cinnamon work so well together. This is one of my favourites!

- Cream the butter and sugar together in a mixing bowl. Add the eggs, beat well and follow with the sifted flour.

- Add the raisins, apples, lemon zest, cinnamon and nutmeg. Stir well.

- Pour into the greased pudding basin and cover with a greased round of baking parchment.

- Take a square of foil, larger than the top of the basin; make a pleat in the centre to allow for any expansion during cooking.

- Place over basin and seal well with string, making sure it is tight. It is advisable to make a handle with string to make it easy to remove the basin from the hot pan in the slow cook

- Place in the slow cooker. Fill with warm water so it reaches half way up the pudding bowl sides. Put on high and cook for 2–3 hours.

- Very carefully remove from the slow cooker.

- Serve with homemade custard or a dollop of creme fraiche.

- Desserts

Healthy swap: You can make this recipe so much healthier by making these small changes. Swap butter for low fat margarine, swap sugar for xylitol or stevia, swap self-raising flour wholewheat/brown self-raising or if you are following a wheat-free diet, opt for Doves Farm Gluten Free Self-Raising flour (and add 30ml of water to the mixture).

Top tip: To serve use low fat creme fraiche, fat-free Greek yoghurt or low fat, low sugar ice-cream.

Egg Custard

Ingredients:
4 eggs
500ml milk
1 tsp cornflour
40g sugar/xylitol
1 tsp vanilla extract
Grated fresh nutmeg
Greased 1.2 litre pudding
  basin

When I was little, my mum always made me egg custard. I never drank milk so she used to try to fill me up with milky puddings – this still remains a favourite of mine when I am feeling under the weather or need an emotional hug. As the slow cooker is different from an oven-cooked egg custard, it makes a pale, almost white egg custard. I use 1–2 teaspoons of vanilla paste as I love the flavour. Delicious served with fruit compote.

- Beat the eggs in a bowl. Place a little of the milk in a cup and add the cornflour to dissolve. Pour this onto the eggs with the remainder of the milk – don't over beat the mixture. Add the sugar and vanilla extract and combine.

- Pour into the ovenproof dish. Grate nutmeg over the top of the pudding.

- Make sure your ovenproof dish fits in your slow cooker.

- Cover the dish with tin foil and ensure it is sealed well – I tie it with string.

- Place the dish in the slow cooker. Fill with warm water to it half fills up to the sides of the ovenproof dish.

- Turn to high and cook for 2–3 hours, until firm.

NB: You can cook these in mini ramekin dishes, which is great for individual puddings. Once cooked, decorate with raspberries for some added colour and zing.

Healthy swap: To make this recipe slightly healthier, you can swap the sugar for xylitol or stevia. For a lower fat version, you could opt for skimmed milk.

Serves 2–4

Winter Fruit Compote

This makes a wonderful dessert, or you can have this as a warm breakfast either on its own, or with homemade porridge.

- Place dried fruit in your slow cooker with all the ingredients apart from the banana.

- Set to low and cook for 4–6 hours.

- Just prior to serving, remove the cinnamon sticks and cloves. Add sliced banana, stir well and serve immediately.

Healthy swap: This is a very healthy compote but if you want it to be sugar-free, swap the sugar for a drizzle of Sweet Freedom Syrup or xylitol.

Ingredients:
75g prunes
75g figs
75g dried apricots
50g raisins or sultanas
30g sliced dried apple rings
350ml water
1 tbsp brown sugar
1 cinnamon stick
4 whole cloves
2 oranges, peeled and sliced
1 orange, zest and juice
1 banana

Serves 4–6

Individual Slow-cooked Blackberry and Apple Upside Down Cake

Ingredients:
100g sugar/xylitol
100g butter/margarine
2 eggs
1 tsp vanilla extract
100g self-raising flour
1–2 Bramley apples
30–50g blackberries
50g butter
50g brown sugar

These individual upside down puddings really look and taste divine. If you prefer one large dessert, you must choose a dish that is totally sealed (not a springform with a loose base) as you are placing the dish in water. Make sure you grease the dish well – you could, for extra security, pop a layer of greaseproof paper on the base to prevent it all sticking.

- Turn your slow cooker to high.

- Place the 100g of butter and 100g of sugar in your mixer and beat until light and fluffy. Gradually add the eggs and vanilla extract. Fold in the sieved flour.

- Find 4–6 ramekin dishes or individual non-stick pots. Grease the pots ready for use. I normally coat with butter then sprinkle with flour to form a seal.

- Heat the 50g of butter and 50g of brown sugar. Place chopped apple and blackberries in the base of your dishes. Pour over the butter/brown sugar syrup – a little in each dish.

- Top this with your cake mix. You can add more apple or blackberries to your cake mix if you want, or just add a few pieces to the top of the dishes. Sprinkle with a touch of brown sugar.

- Desserts

- Place in your slow cooker, add water until they come halfway up the ramekin dishes. Cook for 2–3 hours, or until the sponge is firm to touch. Carefully remove from the slow cooker, taking care not to burn yourself as these dishes are very hot.

- To serve, carefully loosen the sides of the dishes using a knife. Place a plate over the top of the dishes (top side of the plate meeting the top of the dishes as you are turning these out onto the plate). Hold the plate firmly onto the dish and flip over. The cake should come away easily and sit on the plate, apple and blackberry side up.

- Sprinkle with icing sugar, finish with a dollop of cream, creme fraiche or ice-cream. Delicious.

Healthy swap: You can make this recipe so much healthier by making these small changes. Swap butter for low fat margarine, swap sugar for xylitol or stevia, swap self-raising flour wholewheat/brown self raising or if you are following a wheat-free diet, opt for Doves Farm Gluten Free Self-Raising flour (and add 30ml of water to the mixture).

Top tip: To serve use low fat creme fraiche, fat-free Greek yoghurt or low fat, low sugar ice-cream.

Makes 8–10 slices

Apple and Walnut Loaf

Ingredients:
100g butter/margarine
150g sugar xylitol
2 eggs
200g self-raising flour
2 tsp cinnamon powder
50g chopped walnuts
2 cooking apples, peeled and
    chopped

I love apple cakes of any description. The apple chunks combined with cinnamon is delicious. Walnuts are full of Omega 3, antioxidants, B vitamins, magnesium and fibre. Can be served hot or cold.

- Mix butter and sugar together until light and fluffy.

- Add the eggs a little at a time, continue to mix well.

- Add sifted flour and cinnamon powder and combine until thoroughly mixed.

- Add chopped apple and walnuts. When combined thoroughly, prepare your cake tin – I use a 1lb loaf tin for this recipe. Due to variations of sizes of slow cookers, use an ovenproof dish or basin that fits inside your slow cooker. Alternatively, you can grease the lining of your slow cooker and add the batter (same for the bread pudding).

- Make sure you opt for a cake tin that is solid, not the ones with the loose bottom. Grease well or use a cake liner.

- Pour in the mixture and cover with foil, making sure it is secure.

- Place in the slow cooker, pour in boiling water around the edges of the tin ensuring the water reaches no more than halfway up the tin and cook for 3–4 hours on low.

- Be careful when removing the tin from the slow cooker.

- Serve hot or cool on cooling rack before storing in airtight container.

Healthy swap: You can make this recipe so much healthier by making these small changes. Swap butter for low fat margarine, swap sugar for xylitol or stevia, swap self-raising flour for wholewheat/brown self-raising or if you are following a wheat-free diet, opt for Doves Farm Gluten-Free Self-Raising flour (and add 30ml of water to the mixture).

Top tip: To serve use low fat creme fraiche, fat-free Greek yoghurt or low fat, low sugar ice-cream.

Lemon Curd Pudding

Ingredients:
110g butter or low fat margarine
110g sugar or xylitol
2 eggs
130g self-raising flour or Doves Farm Self-raising
Zest of 2 lemons
2 tbsp lemon juice
3–4 tbsp lemon curd
Baking paper, foil and string
Grease 1.2 litre pudding basin

I love lemon puddings. This recipe uses the homemade lemon curd featured in Chapter 13, Preserves, Chutneys and Sauces of this book. Lemon curd is really easy to make and really will impress people so I urge you to give it a try. You can of course use shop bought lemon curd.

- Place the butter, sugar, eggs and flour in a bowl and beat well. If you are using Dove farm, add 30ml of milk to the mixture.

- Beat in the lemon zest and juice.

- Grease the bowl thoroughly before adding the lemon curd to the base.

- Pour into the greased pudding basin and cover with a greased round of baking parchment.

- Take a square of foil, larger than the top of the basin; make a pleat in the centre to allow for any expansion during cooking.

- Place over basin and seal well with string, making sure it is tight. It is advisable to make a handle with string to make it easy to remove the basin from the hot pan in the slow cooker.

- Place pudding in the stoneware and pour boiling water three quarters of the way up the basin.

- Cook for 3 hours until it is cooked – it should spring back when pressed.

Desserts

- Turn upside down to serve.

Healthy swap: You can make this recipe so much healthier by making these small changes. Swap butter for low fat margarine, swap sugar for xylitol or stevia, swap self-raising flour for wholewheat/brown self-raising or if you are following a wheat-free diet, opt for Doves Farm Gluten Free Self-Raising flour (and add 30ml of water to the mixture).

Top tip: To serve use low fat creme fraiche, fat-free Greek yoghurt or low fat, low sugar ice-cream.

Carrot Cake

Ingredients:
400g self-raising flour
2 tsp cinnamon
1 tsp ground coriander
½ tsp grated nutmeg
150g brown sugar
60ml water
80ml light vegetable oil
2 eggs, beaten
200g grated carrots
60g sultanas
30g desiccated coconut

Allow 15 minutes to preheat
your slow cooker.

This has been really successfully cooked in the slow cooker as well as the oven, so experiment to see what texture you prefer.

- Place dry ingredients in your mixer.

- In a separate bowl or jug, mix the oil, water and eggs together. This is only roughly mixed, so don't worry if they stay separated.

- Pour into the dry mixture and whizz to form a batter. Add the grated carrots, sultanas and coconut. Mix well.

- Pour into greased, solid cake tin (see page 144 for tin sizes) – you can place a liner in the cake tin if you prefer. (If cooking in a traditional oven, bake at 180°C for 45–55 minutes, until firm to touch and skewer comes out clean.)

- Place in the slow cooker on a trivet or upturned saucer, pour in boiling water around the edges of the tin ensuring the water reaches no more than halfway up the tin and cook for 4–6 hours on low, or on high for 2–3 hours, or until firm in the centre.

- Cool on cooling rack before storing in airtight container.

Healthy swap: You can make this recipe so much healthier by making these small changes. Swap butter for low fat margarine, swap sugar for xylitol or stevia, swap self-raising flour for wholewheat self-raising or if you are following a wheat-free diet, opt for Doves Farm Gluten Free Self-Raising flour (and add 30ml of water to the mixture).

Top tip: To serve use low fat creme fraiche, fat-free Greek yoghurt or low fat, low sugar ice-cream.

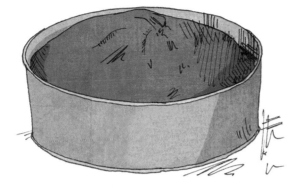

Serves 4–6

Blackberry Layer Sponge Pudding

Ingredients:
100g butter or low fat margarine
100g sugar/xylitol
2 eggs
150g self-raising flour
1 tsp vanilla extract
200g blackberries
Greased 1.2 litre pudding basin

Allow 15 minutes to preheat your slow cooker.

Every year my son and I go out and pick blackberries for the freezer – if you don't have any to hand, why not swap for another berry or a handful of frozen summer fruits.

- Beat the butter and the sugar together until golden. Gradually add the eggs – if it starts to curdle add a touch of the sifted flour.

- Add the sifted flour and continue to beat well. Mix in the vanilla extract.

- Grease your pudding basin. Place a couple of spoonfuls of the sponge mix into the pudding bowl. Add a sprinkling of blackberries, add more sponge mix and continue layering until you reach the top, finish with a layer of sponge mix.

- Cover with baking parchment.

- Take a square of foil, larger than the top of the basin; make a pleat in the centre to allow for any expansion during cooking.

- Place over basin and seal well with string, making sure it is tight. It is advisable to make a handle with string to make it easy to remove the basin from the hot pan in the slow cooker.

- Place the basin in the slow cooker. Add warm water until it comes halfway up the outside of the basin.

● Desserts

- Put on high and cook for 2–3 hours, or until firm to touch.

- Serve with homemade custard or creme fraiche.

Healthy swap: You can make this recipe so much healthier by making these small changes. Swap butter for low fat margarine, swap sugar for xylitol or stevia, swap self-raising flour for wholewheat self-raising or if you are following a wheat-free diet, opt for Doves Farm Gluten Free Self-Raising flour (and add 30ml of water to the mixture).

Top tip: To serve use low fat creme fraiche, fat-free Greek yoghurt or low fat, low sugar ice-cream.

Serves 8–10

Crock Pot Christmas Pudding

Ingredients:
75g plain flour
½ tsp ground nutmeg
¼ tsp mixed spice
75g suet
150g dark brown sugar
150g currants
125g raisins
125g sultanas
25g almonds, roughly
   chopped
100g fresh white
   breadcrumbs
50g mixed peel
1 cooking apple, grated
Grated zest and juice of 1
   lemon
2 eggs, beaten
2 tbsp brandy
Baking paper, foil and string
Grease 1.2 litre pudding basin

This recipe was kindly given to me by Crock Pot – it is the perfect Christmas pudding recipe for using in your slow cooker.

- Sift together the flour, nutmeg and mixed spice in a bowl.

- Add the suet, brown sugar, dried fruit, almonds, breadcrumbs and mixed peel. Mix well.

- Add apple, lemon zest and juice, eggs and brandy. Stir well until all ingredients are well combined.

- Pour into the greased pudding basin and cover with a greased round of baking parchment.

- Take a square of foil, larger than the top of the basin; make a pleat in the centre to allow for any expansion during cooking.

- Place over basin and seal well with string, making sure it is tight. It is advisable to make a handle with string to make it easy to remove the basin from the hot pan in the slow cooker.

- Place pudding in the stoneware and pour boiling water three quarters of the way up the basin. Cook for 8–10 hours on low, the longer the cook, the darker the pudding.

- To reheat the pudding, place in stoneware with boiling water and reheat on high for 3 hours.

● Desserts

NB: The pudding may be made a few months before Christmas, stored in a cool dark place and occasionally fed with brandy.

Healthy swap: Not sure if you should really worry too much about Christmas pudding – a once a year treat. For a wheat-free option, swap the flour for Doves Farm Plain Flour and the breadcrumbs for gluten-free breadcrumbs.

Top tip: You will also have to swap suet for a gluten free suet. Vegetarians need to opt for a vegetarian suet.

Serves 4

Creamy Raspberry Bread and Butter Pudding

Ingredients:
Butter
6–8 slices of bread (stale is
 perfect for this pudding)
300 ml wholemilk
2 eggs
1 tsp vanilla essence
Brown sugar or xylitol
150g raspberries

Allow 15 minutes to preheat
your slow cooker.

This is an alternative to traditional bread and butter pudding. You could swap the raspberries for sultanas, or if you like chocolate, swap for dark chocolate chips and a sprinkle of hazelnuts or pecans.

- Butter the bread slices. Mix the milk, eggs and vanilla essence together.

- Layer the bread, sprinkling with sugar and raspberries in a 1lb pudding basin. When complete, pour over the milk mixture.

- Cover the bread and butter pudding with foil, making sure it is secure.

- Pour hot water in the slow cooker, so it comes no more than halfway up the side of the pudding dish.

- Place on high heat and cook for 2–3 hours.

- Remove carefully and serve with a dollop of cream, creme fraiche or fat-free Greek yoghurt.

Healthy swap: You can still enjoy bread and butter pudding if you are on a wheat-free diet, simply swap the bread for gluten-free. This dish works better using wholemilk but you can use soya or skimmed if you prefer.

Serves 4

Healthy Vanilla Creme Brulee

If you love creme brulee you may think it is full of calories and fat, but you can make a very tasty healthy version which should satisfy your cravings.

- Combine the yoghurt, vanilla paste, egg yolks and cornflour together – I use my hand blender for this.

- Pour this mixture into each of the ramekin dishes.

- Boil the kettle as you need hot water.

- Place the ramekin dishes in the slow cooker.

- Carefully pour boiling water around the edges of the ramekin dishes until it is about halfway up the sides.

- Bake for 2–3 hours on low or until they start to set – they won't be totally firm. Remove and leave to cool. I normally leave these in the fridge for at least 1 hour before serving.

- When ready to serve, sprinkle with brown sugar and using a kitchen blow torch, caramelise the top until it is golden. If you want to avoid sugar, you could drizzle some agave syrup on the top to create a golden sweet topping.

- Serve immediately.

Ingredients:
300ml 0% fat natural Greek yoghurt
1 tsp vanilla extract paste
4 egg yolks
1 heaped tbsp cornflour
4 tbsp brown sugar or Agave syrup
4 ramekin dishes

Allow 15 minutes to preheat your slow cooker.

Serves 4–6

Chocolate Steamed Pudding

A delicious pudding when you want a comforting dessert. Use the best quality dark chocolate you can find, of at least 70% cocoa solids.

Ingredients:
110g plain flour (or Doves Farm Gluten-Free Plain Flour)
1 tsp baking powder (or gluten-free)
30g cocoa
110g sugar or xylitol
1 heaped tsp instant coffee
30ml hot water
100ml milk
1 egg
75g dark chocolate
Baking paper, foil and string
Grease 1.2 litre pudding basin

Allow 15 minutes to preheat your slow cooker.

- Sift the flour, baking powder and cocoa into a bowl. Stir in the sugar.

- In a jug, mix the coffee with 30ml of hot water. Stir well until dissolved. Add the milk and egg and combine well.

- Pour this into the bowl with the dry ingredients. Beat well with your food mixer.

- Melt the dark chocolate. You can melt by placing a bowl on top of a saucepan of hot water – don't let the base of the bowl touch the hot water. Or you could melt in a microwave but be very careful as it can burn very quickly.

- Pour the melted chocolate into the mixture and combine well.

- Pour into the greased pudding basin and cover with a greased round of baking parchment.

- Take a square of foil, larger than the top of the basin; make a pleat in the centre to allow for any expansion during cooking.

- Place over basin and seal well with string, making sure it is tight. It is advisable to make a handle with string to make it easy to remove the basin from the hot pan in the slow cooker.

- Place pudding in the stoneware and pour boiling water three quarters of the way up the basin.

- Cook on high for 3 hours. The sponge should spring back when touched. Be careful not to burn yourself when removing this from the oven.

- Turn out upside down. Serve with homemade custard or for a healthier treat, a few fresh raspberries and some fat-free yoghurt.

Healthy swap: For a sugar-free pudding, swap the sugar for xylitol. If you want to be gluten-free, change the flour to Doves Farm Plain Flour and Gluten-free baking powder.

Pineapple Upside Down Steamed Pudding

Ingredients:
110g butter or low fat
    margarine
110g sugar or xylitol
2 eggs
110g self-raising flour (or
    Doves Farm Self-Raising
    +30ml milk)
1 tsp vanilla extract or paste
1 small tin pineapple rings
    (you will need 4–6 rings)
2 tbsp of golden syrup or
    Agave syrup
Baking paper, foil and string
Grease 1.2 litre pudding basin

Allow 15 minutes to preheat
your slow cooker.

A little twist on the traditional upside down pudding. It works best with pineapple rings but you can use chunks if you are happy with the pineapple being just in the base rather than all around the edge of the bowl Remember to grease well.

- In a bowl, beat the butter and sugar together until light and fluffy.

- Beat in the eggs, followed by the sifted flour. Remember is you are using Dove Farm, add 30ml milk to the mixture. Stir in the vanilla extract.

- Grease your pudding basin well. Place the pineapple rings around the edges of the bowl – one at the bottom and place the others around the edge.

- Pour the syrup around the pineapples – I use Sweet Freedom or Agave syrup which comes in squeezy bottles so this is quite easy.

- Place the cake mixture in the bowl, covering the pineapple rings. Level the top.

- Cover with a greased round of baking parchment.

- Take a square of foil, larger than the top of the basin; make a pleat in the centre to allow for any expansion during cooking.

Desserts

- Place over basin and seal well with string, making sure it is tight. It is advisable to make a handle with string to make it easy to remove the basin from the hot pan in the slow cooker.

- Place pudding in the stoneware and pour boiling water three quarters of the way up the basin.

- Cook for 3 hours on high.

- Turn out upside down and drizzle with a little syrup. Serve with homemade custard or for a healthier treat, some fat-free yoghurt.

Healthy swap: You can make this recipe so much healthier by making these small changes. Swap butter for low fat margarine, swap sugar for xylitol or stevia, swap self-raising flour for wholewheat/brown self-raising or if you are following a wheat-free diet, opt for Doves Farm Gluten Free Self-Raising flour (and add 30ml of water to the mixture). I use agave syrup or Sweet Freedom as they are low GI and don't spike your blood sugar levels.

Top tip: To serve use low fat creme fraiche, fat-free Greek yoghurt or low fat, low sugar ice-cream.

Serves 4–6

Rice Pudding

Ingredients:
1 litre full fat milk
2–3 tbsp sugar or xylitol
80g pudding rice
2–3 tbsp double cream
(optional)
Sprinkle of nutmeg

One of my son's favourite puddings. Adjust the sweetening to taste. This recipe can be doubled up to make Raspberry Rice Brulee – see Chapter 11, Two for One on page 131.

2 for 1

- Place the milk in a saucepan. Heat gently and stir in the sugar and rice. Once hot, transfer to the slow cooker.

- Place on low and cook for 6–8 hours. Remember to stir every now and again as the rice may stick or cook in lumps otherwise.

- Once cooked, you can serve as is with a sprinkle of nutmeg. If you like a creamier pudding, you can stir in a few tablespoons of cream.

Healthy swap: If you are vegan, you could swap the milk for soya milk and add a cartoon of the soya cream to create a creamy consistency and flavour. Instead of sugar, opt for xylitol.

Serves 6–8

Lemon Cheesecake

I love cheesecake. This recipe is for the slow cooker and does work well. You could make this in a large dish but I have found with the variation of shapes and sizes of crock pots it can be difficult to find a dish that fits inside. Using ramekin dishes makes things much easier. If you have a small slow cooker, you may want to half the recipe or make it in two batches.

Ingredients:
6–8 digestive biscuits, crumbled
30g butter or margarine
600g of cream cheese (2 packs)
Zest of 2 lemons
150g xylitol or sugar
2 eggs, beaten
Lemon curd
6–8 ramekin dishes

- Place the butter in a saucepan and melt. Add the digestive biscuits and coat well with the butter. Remove from the heat and place into your greased ramekin dishes. Press down firmly.

- Mix the remaining ingredients well, apart from the eggs, with a mixer. Add one egg at a time, mixing well in between.

- Pour this into the ramekin dishes, don't overfill as they need room, plus you will be needing a gap at the top as you will add some lemon curd before serving. You can cover with foil if you are concerned about condensation dripping on the cheesecakes – this depends on your cooker as some produce more than others.

- Place in the slow cooker. Fill with hot water to just under halfway up the sides of the ramekin dishes.

- Cook on high for 2–2½ hours. The cheesecake should feel like it is setting well. You can cook on low for 5–6 hours.

- Leave to cool. Cover the tops of the cheesecakes with lemon curd. Place in the fridge to chill before serving.

Serves 4–6

Poached Rhubarb

Ingredients:
1kg rhubarb, cut into 3–4cm
  lengths
100g sugar (or more if you like
  it sweeter) or xylitol
200ml orange juice
Zest of 1 orange
50ml Creme De Cassis liqueur
  (optional but worth it!)
1 vanilla pod

I love rhubarb and this recipe really enhances the flavours – a posh stewed rhubarb! This recipe can be doubled up to make a delicious Nutty Rhubarb Crumble and Rhubarb and Ginger Upside Down Cake – see Chapter 11, Two for One on page 132.

2 for 1

- Place everything in the slow cooker.

- Cook on high for 1½–2 hours until the rhubarb is soft but still holds its shape.

- Serve hot or cold.

- This is delicious with porridge for breakfast, or with yoghurt.

Healthy swap: Swap the sugar for xylitol.

Desserts

Serves 4

Baked Apples

A traditional autumnal treat that is really easy to prepare. Serve with ice-cream, custard or a healthy dollop of low-fat Greek yoghurt.

Ingredients:
4 Bramley apples, cored but
    not peeled
3–4 tbsp mincemeat
250ml apple juice or water

- Wash and core your apples, leaving the skins intact.

- Stuff the cores of the apples with the mincemeat.

- Place in the base of your slow cooker. Pour the apple juice around the apples. Cook on high for 2–3 hours until the apples are soft.

- Serve with low fat creme fraiche or natural yoghurt.

Serves 4–6

Lemon Saucy Pudding

Ingredients:
100g butter/low fat margarine
175g sugar/xylitol
Juice and zest of 3 lemons
4 eggs, separated
1 tsp vanilla essence or paste
250ml milk
50g plain flour
4–6 ramekin dishes

Allow 15 minutes to preheat your slow cooker.

This is a really light pudding that is quite addictive. The soufflé-like sponge sits on top of a zingy lemon sauce. Delicious.

- Beat the butter and sugar together until creamy.

- Mix the lemon zest into the beaten sugar/butter mixture.

- Add the egg yolks, vanilla and lemon juice. Beat well before adding the flour and milk.

- This will form a quite runny batter. Give it a thorough stir to make sure the mixer has not left anything on the edges.

- Meanwhile, in a clean bowl, beat the egg whites until they form soft peaks.

- Fold this into the batter gently.

- Grease your individual ramekin dishes with butter. Pour in the mixture.

- In your slow cooker, fill with hot water up to approximately 3cm (1inch) from the bottom.

- Add the ramekin dishes so the water comes halfway up their sides.

- Cook on high for 1 hour, then check. The pudding should have a golden sponge topping which is firm to touch. Depending on your slow cooker it should take between 1 and 1½ hours to cook.

- Desserts

- When you serve the pudding, you will notice the bottom half is a gooey lemon sauce and the top should be a lovely light sponge.

- Serve with creme fraiche or Greek yoghurt.

Mulled Poached Pears

Ingredients:
4–6 ripe pears
350–500ml mulled wine
2 oranges, thickly sliced
175g sugar or xylitol

Serve with vanilla ice-cream or a dollop of creme fraiche. This recipe can be doubled up to make Pear and Chocolate Upside Down Cake – see Chapter 11, Two for One on page 134.

2 for 1

- Place the wine in a saucepan and heat up gently. Add the sugar and stir until dissolved.

- Peel your pears retaining the stalk if possible. Cut the bottom off the pear allowing it to stand without falling over.

- Slice the oranges – do not peel. Place the orange slices in the bottom of the slow cooker.

- Place the pears in the slow cooker – you can sit the pears upright on top of the orange slices or lie flat to allow more of the pears to be covered in the liquid.

- Pour the wine over the pears.

- Cook for 3–4 hours until the pears are soft.

- Place the pears on a plate and drizzle over with the juice. Serve with a dollop of cream, Greek yoghurt or creme fraiche.

Healthy swap: If you want to cut down on sugar, swap this for xylitol or stevia – be aware that stevia is very sweet so you will need much less.

Top tip: You can also buy alcohol free mulled wine for a less calorific option.

Serves 6–8

Plum Clafoutis

Clafoutis is a French dessert traditionally made with black cherries. It is more of an egg custard top rather than a sponge. I made this one day when I had some extra ripe plums and did not know what to do with them. It was a big hit with the family. This recipe uses full fat milk. If you aren't worried about the extra calories, you can use half milk, half double cream.

Ingredients:
6–8 ripe plums, halved and
  stoned
300ml of full fat milk
25g butter or margarine
3 egg yolks
2 whole eggs
1 tsp vanilla extract
120g sugar/xylitol
50g ground almonds
50g plain flour

- Remove the pan from the slow cooker and grease well with butter. Place the plums in the base of the slow cooker.

- Heat the milk, butter and vanilla extract in a pan – do not allow it to boil. Remove and allow to cool once the butter has melted into the milk.

- In a bowl, beat the eggs, yolks and sugar together until light and fluffy. Add the almonds and flour to the egg mixture and combine well – gradually adding the milk mixture to form a batter.

- Pour this over the plums.

- Place on high and cook for 2½–3½ hours – the top should be a light spongy egg custard.

- Serve immediately with cream or ice-cream.

Makes 4–6 mugs

Hot Chocolate Orange Brownie Mugs

Ingredients:
110g self-raising flour
100g brown sugar or xylitol
75g cocoa
150ml orange juice
100ml sunflower oil
25g dark chocolate chips
Spray olive oil
4–6 ovenproof mugs

A friend of mine made these and they were a big hit with everyone. It really is a hug in a mug.

- To prepare the brownie mix, add all the dry ingredients into your food mixer. Measure the oil and orange juice and mix together.

- Pour this into the dried mix and beat well until thoroughly mixed.

- Stir in by hand the chocolate chips, ensuring they are evenly distributed.

- Make sure your mugs are dishwasher and microwave proof – normally the chunkier mugs are suitable – not fine bone china.

- Carefully spray with oil the insides of the mugs (you can rub with butter, then sprinkle on flour to form a non-stick base).

- Fill the mugs half full with the mixture.

- Boil the kettle as you need hot water to place around the mugs.

- Turn the slow cooker to high. Carefully place the mugs in the slow cooker and fill the slow cooker with hot water until it comes just over halfway up the outside of the mugs. Cook for 2 hours – or until the brownies have risen and firm to touch.

- Very carefully remove the mugs from the slow cooker – use oven gloves for this. Carefully hold the mugs at the top and run the handles under cold water – this will cool them enough for you to be able to hold them.

- Serve hot – you can decorate with cream or creme fraiche before serving.

Healthy swap: For those following a gluten-free diet, you can swap the flour for a self-raising gluten-free flour – I use Doves Farm. Add 30ml of milk to the mixture.

Top tip: If you want to cut down on the sugar, switch to xylitol or stevia.

Gooseberry Fool

Ingredients:
500g gooseberries, washed
100ml water
50g sugar (or more if you like it sweeter) or xylitol
250ml thick double cream
250ml thick natural Greek yoghurt

I adore gooseberries. I try to freeze them when in season so they last a bit longer. You can follow this recipe for rhubarb fool. Simply swap the gooseberries for rhubarb and follow as described.

- Place the gooseberries and water in the slow cooker. Place on high and cook for 2–3 hours, until they are soft and pop when pressed with a spoon.

- Remove and leave to cool.

- When cool mix with the cream and yoghurt.

- Chill before serving.

Healthy swap: This recipe uses half cream, half Greek yoghurt. If you want to cut down the calories, you can opt for all Greek yoghurt.

Top tip: To cut down on sugar, use xylitol or stevia.

Preserves, Chutneys and Sauces

CHAPTER
13

There is nothing nicer than making your own jams, chutneys, curds and sauces. One of the benefits of the slow cooker is the lack of smell. If you have made chutneys before, you will know that the smell seems to seep into every room of the house and before you know it, your home has the smell of spiced vinegar for days. The slow cooker seals in the smell, so perfect for chutneys and pickling vegetables such as beetroot. Jams and marmalades need a rapid boil to set so you have to transfer to a pan for this final stage.

Sterilise

Before you start cooking preserves or chutneys, you really need to sterilise your jars. You can opt to do this in your dishwasher or you can use the more traditional technique, see below.

- Wash the jars thoroughly in warm clean soapy water, rinse and drain upside down on kitchen towel and place on a baking tray or direct onto rack (if using an oven rack, take care when you remove them).

- Place into preheated oven at 100°C or gas 1 for 15 minutes. Turn the oven to its lowest setting to keep jars warm while you make chutney. When removing jars from the oven, place onto an old newspaper or tea towel. Be careful not to touch the inside of the jars as you will contaminate them.

Storage

All the sauces in this chapter can be frozen or stored in an air-tight container in the fridge for up to one week. Chutneys can be stored for up to three months if prepared in sterilised jars. If curds are placed in sterilised jars, the can last up to three months if kept in a refrigerator unopened, six weeks in a cool, dark place but only about a week once opened – I tend to pop the curds into very small jars to avoid wastage.

Note: For all of the recipes in this chapter, **if your slow cooker needs to be preheated, turn it on 15 minutes before using.** Refer to your manufacturer's instructions for more information on your specific model temperatures.

Preserves, Chutneys and Sauces

Slow-cooked Fruit and Chilli Chutney

- Turn your slow cooker to high.

- Place all the ingredients in the saucepan. Bring to the boil and simmer for 5 minutes.

- Transfer to your slow cooker and cook for 4 hours, stirring occasionally.

- When you have achieved the right consistency, place into sterilised jars. Cover with waxed paper and store for at least 1 month.

Ingredients:
600g red onions
600g Bramley apples
200g pears
200g plums
150g sultanas
50g ginger
2-3 chillies (depending on
    your personal taste)
750g sugar
450ml white wine vinegar

Red Onion Marmalade

Ingredients:
2–3 tbsp olive oil
20g butter
450g red onions, sliced
3 tbsp dark brown sugar
50g sultanas
1 tsp paprika
200ml red wine
40ml balsamic vinegar
Seasoning to taste

This is a huge favourite of mine. Delicious served with cheese on toast, or why not use this as your base for a red onion and goats cheese tart. You can cook this in a casserole dish, preserving pan or your slow cooker.

- Heat the oil in a sauté pan. Add the onions and the butter. Cook until the onions are soft and translucent. Add the sugar, stir well.

- Place in your slow cooker and set to hot. Leave for 1 hour.

- Add the remaining ingredients and leave for another 2 hours.

- Add seasoning and adjust to taste – you may want to add more sugar or balsamic vinegar to suit your palate.

- Cook for another 30 minutes or until the marmalade liquid has reduced, but not dried.

- Season and store in the fridge until needed.

Preserves, Chutneys and Sauces

Mum's Tomato Chutney

- Place all ingredients in a preserving pan or large deep saucepan
  add half the vinegar and seasoning (salt and pepper).

- Place the pan over a medium heat, slowly bring to a simmer stirring constantly until the sugar has dissolved.

- Transfer into the slow cooker and set to low and cook for 6–8 hours or until it has reached your desired thickness.

- Divide the chutney between the sterilised jars and allow to cool – I do this with a ladle and a measuring jug – take care as it is very hot and will splash as you fill the jars.

- When cool, place a waxed disc onto each jar and seal with airtight lids or cellophane and elastic bands. Store in a cool dry place for 1 month to allow to mature. When opened keep in the fridge and use with 2 months.

Ingredients:
1kg ripe tomatoes, chopped
450g onions, chopped
2 garlic cloves, finely chopped
2 cooking apples, peeled cored and chopped
2 tsp mustard seed or mustard powder
small piece of fresh ginger grated about 3 cm long
300g sultanas
200g light muscavado sugar
600 ml spiced vinegar (or malt will do if you cannot find ready spiced or you can buy spices and spice your own)

Slow-cooked Fruity Chutney

Ingredients:

3 onions, finely chopped
3–4 cloves garlic, crushed
3 inch knuckle of fresh ginger, grated
3 ripe peaches, chopped
3 ripe pears, chopped
2 apples, chopped
200g sultanas
50g raisins
200g sugar
1 tsp ground cinnamon
1 tsp allspice
4 tsp wholegrain mustard
500 ml vinegar

If you have a fruit bowl with some over-ripe fruit, why not turn it into a tasty chutney? Combine these ingredients in your slow cooker for a simple, yet yummy chutney.

- Place all ingredients in slow cooker. Turn to low and cook for 5–6 hours, until mixture is right consistency ready to bottle as instructed in previous chutney recipes.

- If you prefer to cook this in a preserving pan, place all ingredients in the pan and cook on medium heat for 1 hour before bottling in your sterilised and prepared jars.

Slow-cooked Cranberry Sauce

Get into the Christmas spirit and make this amazing sauce, the whole house will smell wonderfully Christmassy. This is an alcohol-free sauce – if you want something with a little more kick, have a look at my Boozy Cranberry Sauce recipe on page 183.

Ingredients:
500g cranberries
1 cooking apple, chopped
250ml water
Zest of 1 orange
150g sugar
2–3 tsp ground cinnamon

- Place all ingredients in the slow cooker, stir well to ensure it is blended. Turn the cooker to high and cook for 3–4 hours, stirring occasionally.

- Place in serving dish or in jars until ready to use.

Makes approx. 2 jars

Lemon Curd

Ingredients:
100g butter
175–250g caster sugar
(depends on how sweet
you like it)
Zest and juice of 4 large
lemons (removing any pips)
4 eggs
1.2 litre pudding basin

I love lemon curd. I use it to sandwich my lemon sponge together, alongside a layer of buttercream. I also add a dollop to the centre of lemon cupcakes. My son loves it on toast, so all in all, it is a vital ingredient in the Flower household.

- Place the butter, sugar, lemon zest and juice in your pudding basin. Place in the slow cooker and turn to high. Place boiling water around the bowl until it comes up halfway.

- Leave for 20 minutes. Remove from the slow cooker and leave to cool for 5 minutes. Keep the slow cooker on as you will be returning the basin back shortly.

- Beat the eggs and pour this, whilst continuing to beat, though a sieve, into the lemon mixture.

- Take a square of foil, larger than the top of the basin. Place over basin and seal well with string, making sure it is tight.

- Place back into the slow cooker keeping the temperature high. Add more boiling water around the basin, ensuring the water comes up over halfway up the bowl.

- Cook for 1½–2½ hours, stirring a couple of times to avoid any lumps (if you forget to stir and it goes lumpy or curdles, whisk well with a balloon whisk).

- The curd should be thick enough to hold when poured from the back of a spoon, but not thick and lumpy.

Preserves, Chutneys and Sauces

- Pour into your sterilised jars. Cover with a layer of parchment before sealing with the lid.

- Keep refrigerated once opened.

NB: If you want a more grown up curd, simply add 30–50ml of Limoncello to the mix. Do this halfway through cooking – any earlier and it might curdle.

Healthy tip: The sugar content here suits people who like a tart and not overly sweet-tasting lemon curd. Although this recipe has a high level of sugar, you are only going to use a small amount per portion.

Top tip: I have also made this with a stevia blend (half stevia half sugar such as Tate & Lyles Light at Heart) and it has worked well at 125g. Because the stevia is very sweet, this is plenty.

All-purpose Tomato Base

Ingredients:
1kg tomatoes, chopped
1 large red onion, chopped
2–3 cloves of garlic, roughly
  chopped
1 red pepper, diced
150ml red wine or stock
½ tsp dried thyme
½ tsp dried oregano
1 tsp dried parsley
1 tsp sugar
Sprinkle of salt and pepper
1 tsp balsamic vinegar
  (optional)

This is a real gem and so easy to make. Perfect for using up overripe tomatoes or when you see tomatoes on offer in the supermarket. You can make this in a saucepan – if so, you would use fresh herbs, but the slow cooker is so easy. Feel free to change the herbs to suit your own preference.

- Add all the ingredients and combine well.

- Set the temperature to low and cook for 8–10 hours.

- When cooled, freeze or store in the fridge in an airtight container for up to 3–4 days.

Recipe tips: This base can be used as a pasta sauce, base for a bolognaise or lasagne, topping for pizza or base for any Italian inspired dish. I always seem to have a container of this in my fridge. When I can't be bothered to cook a big meal, I simply sauté an onion and pepper, add the base sauce and a tin or two of mixed beans. Served topped with crumbled feta – delicious!

Spicy Apple Sauce

This is delicious with cheese and biscuits or can be used with pork dishes.

- Place all ingredients in the slow cooker. Combine well.

- Cook on low for 4–5 hours.

- Place in airtight container or sterilised jars.

Ingredients:
5 apples (Bramley work well),
    peeled and diced
1 onion, diced
100g sultanas
2cm knuckle of ginger, finely
    chopped
1 tsp cinnamon
1 tsp ground coriander
2 tsp lemon juice
200ml spiced vinegar
150g sugar or xylitol

Marrow and Vegetable Chutney

Ingredients:
500ml spiced vinegar
500g cooking apple, peeled and chopped
2 large red or orange peppers, chopped and seeded
300g sugar
180g raisins or sultanas
300g onion, diced
½ large marrow or 4 large courgettes, peeled seeded and chopped
1 small chilli, seeded and chopped
2 cloves garlic, crushed
1 tsp turmeric
1 tsp cumin
1–2 tsp mild curry powder
1 tsp salt

You can use any vegetables for this – it is great if you grow your own vegetables and want to use up any less than perfect vegetables.

- Place all the ingredients in the saucepan. Bring to the boil and simmer for 5 minutes.

- Transfer to your slow cooker and cook on high for 4 hours, stirring occasionally.

- When you have achieved the right consistency, place into sterilised jars. Cover with waxed paper and store for at least 1 month.

Boozy Cranberry Sauce

I love this – I make it every Christmas, but must admit to messing about with the recipe to suit what booze I have in the cupboard. I am a bit of a nightmare when cooking as I don't weigh things, so I had to make this again to get the right quantities for you all. I don't like overly sweet sauces, so I tend to use very little sugar – feel free to adjust this to suit your own palate. Add the smaller amount of sugar to start. Cook for half the time, then taste (carefully as it will be hot) and adjust sweetness to taste. The cranberry sauce will thicken slightly when cool.

Ingredients:
500g cranberries
100ml port
100ml vodka
Zest and juice of 1 orange
Zest of 1 lemon
½ tsp allspice
75g sugar (or to taste) or xylitol

- Place all the ingredients in the slow cooker.

- Cook for 2–3 hours until the cranberries are starting to pop and collapse.

- Store in jars or sterilised bottles until needed – should last about 1 month in the fridge in a sealed jar.

Apple and Blackberry Curd

Ingredients:
900g blackberries
300g apples
100g butter
250g caster sugar (more if
  you like it very sweet) or
  xylitol
4 eggs
1.2 litre pudding basin

I was looking for things to do with blackberries and found this recipe in a scrapbook of recipes given to me years ago by an elderly neighbour. It was in note form so I had to play around to make sense of it all but the result was really yummy. My son loves this swirled into yoghurt.

- Stew the apple and blackberries until the fruit is soft – only use a very small amount of water when stewing as you don't want the stewed fruit to be too wet. Push through a sieve to remove any pips – it is nice to have a really smooth curd.

- Place the butter, sugar in your pudding basin. Place in the slow cooker and turn to high. Place boiling water around the bowl until it comes up halfway.

- Leave for 20 minutes. Remove from the slow cooker and leave to cool for 5 minutes. Keep the slow cooker on as you will be returning the basin back shortly.

- Mix the fruit puree in with the butter/sugar mixture.

- Beat the eggs and pour this, whilst continuing to beat, though a sieve, into the mixture.

- Take a square of foil, larger than the top of the basin. Place over basin and seal well with string, making sure it is tight.

- Place back into the slow cooker keeping the temperature high. Add more boiling water around the basin, ensuring the water comes up over halfway up the bowl.

- Cook for 1 ½–2 ½ hours, stirring a couple of times to avoid any lumps (if you forget to stir and it goes lumpy or curdles, whisk well with a balloon whisk).

- The curd should be thick enough to hold when poured from the back of a spoon, but not thick and lumpy.

- Pour into your sterilised jars. Cover with a layer of parchment before sealing with the lid.

- Keep refrigerated once opened.

NB: If you want a more grown up curd, simply add 30–50ml of cointreau to the mix. Do this halfway through cooking – any earlier and it might curdle.

Makes approx. 6 jars

Mum's Seville Orange Marmalade

Ingredients:
600g Seville oranges
1 large lemon
1 litre water
500g sugar (I use granulated
   but you could use
   preserving sugar)

Traditionally Seville oranges are used to make marmalade (these are in season at the beginning of the year). They are small, very sour oranges the appearance of which is not as nice as normal sweet oranges. However, marmalade can be made from almost all citrus fruits or a mixture of several, e.g. orange, orange and lemon, lemon and lime or grapefruit. Clementine or satsuma will give a very sweet marmalade more like a jam. The peel takes a while to soften so it ideal for the slow cooker – peel is cooked until it is softened. I do this the day before and allow it to cool for safety reasons adding the sugar the next day and finishing the process – although if you are really careful, it could be done in one day.

- Wash the fruit to get rid of any dirt or coatings.

- Quarter the oranges and remove all the pith and the pips (do so over a bowl or tray to retain all the juice). All the fruit is used when making marmalade, including the peel, pith and pips, as these help to give a good set.

- Place the pith and pips into a muslin bag and tie tightly.

- Pour any juice into the slow cooker add the water.

- Slice the peel to the required size – thick or thin depending on your personal preference (best done on a chopping board with a sharp knife).

- Place peel into the cooker, lay the muslin bag on the top and cook on high for 4–5 hours stirring occasionally.

Preserves, Chutneys and Sauces

- Test that the peel is softened if not cook for another hour. Allow to cool.

- Next day pour the mixture into a large saucepan or preserving pan if you have one heat until simmering. Add sugar and stir over heat until the sugar has dissolved.

- Bring to the boil and boil rapidly for 10 minutes.

- Test for setting by putting a teaspoon full onto a cold plate and after 10 minutes gently push the liquid with your index finger. If small creases are made on the skin of the sample it is ready to put into jars. If not, repeat the setting test. Marmalade takes longer to set than other jams.

- When set, pour into sterilised jars and this should make about 6 jars.

Top tip: When marmalade is cooking, a large amount of scum will form on the surface. Add approximately a level teaspoon of butter and stir and this will remove most of it. Skim off remainder with a slotted spoon.

Orange and Whiskey Marmalade

Ingredients:
600g oranges
1 large lemon
900ml water
50ml whiskey
500g sugar (I use granulated but you could use preserving sugar)

A variation to the marmalade recipe – you can add more whiskey if you prefer a stronger flavour.

- Wash the fruit to get rid of any dirt or coatings.

- Quarter the oranges and remove all the pith and the pips (do so over a bowl or tray to retain all the juice). All the fruit is used when making marmalade, including the peel, pith and pips, as these help to give a good set.

- Place the pith and pips into a muslin bag and tie tightly.

- Pour any juice into the slow cooker add the water.

- Slice the peel to the required size – thick or thin depending on your personal preference (best done on a chopping board with a sharp knife).

- Place peel into the cooker, lay the muslin bag on the top and cook on high for 4–5 hours stirring occasionally.

- Test that the peel is softened if not cook for another hour. Allow to cool.

- Next day pour the mixture into a large saucepan or preserving pan if you have one heat until simmering. Add sugar and whiskey and stir over heat until the sugar has dissolved.

- **Preserves, Chutneys and Sauces**

- Bring to the boil and boil rapidly for 10 minutes.

- Test for setting by putting a teaspoon full onto a cold plate and after 10 minutes gently push the liquid with your index finger. If small creases are made on the skin of the sample it is ready to put into jars. If not, repeat the setting test. Marmalade takes longer to set than other jams.

- When set pour into sterilised jars. This should make about 6 jars.

Pickled Beetroot

Ingredients:
Beetroot
Water

You can pickle this beetroot or use fresh cooked in dishes such as a salad, salsa or as a side dish. There are no real quantities here as it depends how big the beetroot is and the size of your slow cooker. If you grow your own beetroot this is a great way to cook it as you get no smell.

- Wash and trim the beetroot. Leave about 2–3cm of stalk on the beetroot otherwise they bleed.

- Place in the slow cooker and cover with water.

- Cook for 5–6 hours – times depend on size of the beetroot. Test to see if they are cooked – use a sharp knife and you can gauge how soft they are.

- Remove from the slow cooker. If you want to pickle them, slice or dice, or if baby beetroot they can be left whole after the remaining stalks have been removed. Place in your sterilised jars and pour on malt vinegar.

NB: Throw in a few juniper berries with the water to add a lovely flavour to the beetroot.

Red Cabbage

Serve this hot as a vegetable side dish (perfect at Christmas too) or store in sterilised jars.

- Place all the ingredients in the slow cooker.

- Cook on low for 8 hours.

- Serve hot or cold.

Ingredients:
1 red cabbage, finely shredded
1 large apple, peeled and diced
1 small red onion, finely chopped
½ tsp allspice
150ml red wine vinegar

Makes approx. 2 jars

Orange Curd

Ingredients:
100g butter
175–250g caster sugar (depends on how sweet you like it) or xylitol
Zest and juice of 3 large oranges (removing any pips)
Zest and juice of 1 lemon
4 eggs
1.2 litre pudding basin

This is a really lovely alternative to lemon curd. Just like lemon, I use it a lot for cooking – mixing in with yoghurt, filling a cake or as a base to a sponge pudding.

- Place the butter, sugar, zest and juice in your pudding basin. Place in the slow cooker and turn to high. Place boiling water around the bowl until it comes up halfway.

- Leave for 20 minutes. Remove from the slow cooker and leave to cool for 5 minutes. Keep the slow cooker on as you will be returning the basin back shortly.

- Beat the eggs and pour this, whilst continuing to beat, though a sieve, into the curd mixture.

- Take a square of foil, larger than the top of the basin. Place over basin and seal well with string, making sure it is tight.

- Place back into the slow cooker keeping the temperature high. Add more boiling water around the basin, ensuring the water comes up over halfway up the bowl.

- Cook for 1½–2½ hours, stirring a couple of times to avoid any lumps (if you forget to stir and it goes lumpy or curdles, whisk well with a balloon whisk).

- The curd should be thick enough to hold when poured from the back of a spoon, but not thick and lumpy.

Preserves, Chutneys and Sauces

- Pour into your sterilised jars. Cover with a layer of parchment before sealing with the lid.

- Keep refrigerated once opened.

NB: If you want a more luxurious curd, why not make a orange and cointreau curd. Simply add 30–50ml of cointreau to the mix. Do this halfway through cooking – any earlier and it might curdle.

Healthy tip: The sugar content here suits people who like a tart and not overly sweet-tasting curd. Although this recipe has a high level of sugar, you are only going to use a small amount per portion.

Top tip: I have also made this with a stevia blend (half stevia half sugar such as Tate & Lyles Light at Heart) and it has worked well at 125g. Because the stevia is very sweet, this is plenty.

Plum Jam

Ingredients:
3kg plums, halved (keep stones intact)
3kg sugar
360ml water

You can use granulated sugar in this recipe as plums have high pectin.

- Place plums and water in the slow cooker and cook on high for 2 hours.

- The stones help it to set and should float to the top. You can remove them with a metal slotted spoon.

- You can transfer this straight into a preserving pan but be very careful as it will be very hot so may be better to allow the mixture to cool – you could leave in the cooker till the next day if you prefer.

- Transfer to a saucepan or preserving pan and add the sugar. Stir until dissolved.

- Allow to rapid boil for 10 minutes.

- Remove any scum on the top with a slotted spoon and discard.

- Pour a spoonful onto a cold plate and test for setting.

- When setting point is reached, allow to cool slightly before pouring into sterilised jars.

Homemade Stock

I am not a fan of stock cubes – I find they are much too salty and quite overpowering. I do occasionally use the Knorr Stock Pot Gels, but again, use with care as they are very salty. I prefer homemade stock and often find water and a good selection of herbs and spices does the trick. Making your own stock is not as time consuming as it sounds. The joy of the slow cooker is it keeps the smell in and you can leave it to do all the work while you get on with your life. Perfect for using any leftover and almost gone-off vegetables. Bottle it in the fridge or freeze until required.

Vegetable Stock

There really is no recipe for stock, anything goes. I normally raid my vegetable drawer and pull out anything that is really not suitable for fresh vegetable dishes any more. I also include some of the bits of veg we would normally throw away, which I have saved up over a few days, as it still has lots of flavour. Don't use anything from the Brassica family as it will make your stock smell – so no cauliflower, cabbage, broccoli, etc.

- Place your chosen ingredients in a stock pan and cover with water. Add any chosen herbs and seasoning.

- Cook for up to 8 hours on low.

- Strain and retain the liquid. Bottle in the fridge for up to 4 days or freeze for up to 3 months.

Meat and Fish Stock

When making a meat or fish stock, you can use the bones of the carcasses and even the heads of the fish, so there is no waste. Add wine and vegetables that suit the stock you are making. If making a meat stock, stick to one animal or bird source. Remember to strain thoroughly before bottling. Label and date stock, especially if you are placing this in the freezer.

- Place your chosen ingredients in a stock pan and cover with water. Add any chosen herbs and seasoning.

- Cook for up to 8 hours on low.

- Strain and retain the liquid. Bottle in the fridge for up to 4 days or freeze for up to 3 months.

Preserves, Chutneys and Sauces

Index